Mr. Mackay's Legacy

St. John's School in Perth (1832-2010)

Brian Toner

Anna Books

First published in Great Britain in 2010 by
Anna Books
Gayfield, Perth Road,
Pitlochry PH16 5LY

A CIP catalogue record for this book is available from the British Library.

ISBN   978-0-9564956-0-0

Printed by
Wm Culross & Son Limited
Coupar Angus, Perthshire,
Scotland   PH13 9DF

Contents

Preface & Acknowledgements   v

Introduction: Before 1832   1

1   A Destitute Parish (1832-1856)   3

2   An Ample Supply of Slate Pencils (1856-1872)   7

3   Payment by Results (1872-1901)   19

4   Problems Galore (1901-1937)   31

Interlude: The Name's the Same   43

5   This Magnificent School (1938)   45

6   Wartime (1939-1945)   53

7   Overcrowding and Beyond (1945-1967)   63

8   From One School, Make Three (1967-1980)   83

9   Struggling Through (1980-2005)   93

10   New Century, New School (2005 onwards)   117

Appendices   123

  Head Teachers of St. John's School (1860-2010)

  Head Teachers of St. Columba's High School (1967-2009)

  Parish Priests of St. John's Catholic Parish (1830-2010)

  Former Pupils of St. John's who fell during World War I

Bibliography   127

Photograph Credits   128

Index   129

**Author's note on titles of clergy, currency values
and churches dedicated to St. John the Baptist**

In my use of titles for clergymen, I have followed the conventions of the time. The title of 'Father' was not given to Catholic priests until the late nineteenth century and the St. John's story starts in the pre-Victorian period with priests known as 'Mr.' Senior clergy were addressed as 'Dr.' although whether that indicated the university degree of Doctor of Divinity, or simply an honorary title, I am not always sure. Perhaps it varied from person to person.

Prices have remained in the values of their time and are written in £sd or pounds, shillings and pence. Six pounds, four shillings and eleven pence is £6/4/11 while eight pounds, seven shillings is £8/7/-.

There are various devices available for converting historical sums of money to present values but they are not straightforward. Some conversions reflect wages, others are based on prices and depending on which you choose, the results can vary dramatically.

There are three churches named after St. John the Baptist in Perth. The main pre-Reformation church in the city centre, I refer to as *St John's Kirk*. The other one I mention is the Catholic *Church of St. John the Baptist* in Melville Street which was particularly important to the early years of this story.

Preface and Acknowledgements

St. John's School began its life in Perth in the most unpromising of circumstances. Today it's the oldest surviving school in the city after Perth Academy and, as I write, work is proceeding on the building which will become the school's next home: bigger, better and shinier than ever.

My interest in the school's history was fired by my discovery, in a seldom-used cupboard, of a stack of dusty, leather-bound log books. Many dated from the nineteenth century. The head teachers who wrote them are long gone but reading about their problems and successes brought home to me that St. John's School is a long-running and fascinating story. The hope that others might find the story interesting too, encouraged me to write *Mr. Mackay's Legacy*.

At this point I should mention former pupils, Charles Sweeney (resident in Perth) and Edward Lang (resident in Canada). As well as having gone through St. John's (1942-52), they visited me together, some years ago, and regaled me with memories of their schooldays. I think this meeting was the final encouragement to produce an account of St. John's history.

Preparing the story for publication required the help of many individuals who have been generous with their knowledge, expertise, time and enthusiasm.

Bernadette Scott, head teacher of St. John's Primary School (2005-2009), allowed me access to documents and photographs; Danny O'Donnell read and commented on an early version of the manuscript and introduced me to Canon Michael Lavelle's 1907 book, *A Historical Sketch of the Perth Mission*; David Watson of Ballinluig, taught me about the Perthshire rural economy; Stephen Clayes generously offered me his fascinating archive of the history of St. John's parish; Roben Antoniewicz designed the cover and improved some old photographs; Bernard McMenemy and Andrew Mitchell, at St. Columba's High School, provided photographs and background information.

Photographs are central to this book and I am particularly indebted to the individuals who have allowed me to reproduce copyright works freely: Alison Lowson, editor of the Perthshire Advertiser; Bill McLoughlin at D C Thomson, Dundee; Louis Flood, photographers, Perth; Hazel Adams, Schools' Liaison Officer at Laing O'Rourke and H. Tempest, photographers, St. Ives, Cornwall. It has not been possible to trace the origins of some photographs but information which becomes available will be acknowledged in any future edition of this book

The greatest part of my research has been conducted in the A K Bell Library, Perth. In the Local Studies section I found unstinting enthusiasm and practical advice from librarian, Sara Kelly, while staff at the Perth and Kinross Council archive responded in a most professional manner to my requests for obscure documents and plans.

Perhaps the most important contribution to *Mr. Mackay's Legacy* has come from the former pupils and staff who provided memories and missing photographs: Helen Ford, Frank Gloak, Norma Guillianotti, Michael Lafferty, Rose Mackle, Terry Mason, Irena Miller (Burnett), Yvonne Pirie (Devaney), Pat Rattray, Lawson Smith, Andrew Taylor.

Thanks also to *The Courier*, the *Perthshire Advertiser* and Monsignor Charles Hendry, then parish priest of St. John's, for publishing my original requests for help.

The support of my wife, Judith, was essential. She has been a perceptive sounding board for my ideas and her teacher's eagle eye has made proof reading easy. Nor must I forget our Alaskan Malamute, Anna, whose appetite for long walks has allowed me the space to reorganise my thoughts many times over.

Of course, any errors in this account are my responsibility alone and will be corrected in any future edition.

I hope you enjoy reading *Mr. Mackay's Legacy.*

Brian Toner
January 2010

The Earliest Writing from St. John's

Extract from the first official logbook for St. John's School, Perth. It covers the week, April 11th - 14th, 1864 and was written by the headmistress, Miss Mary Cattanach.

St. John's School and its sites in central Perth (1832-2010)

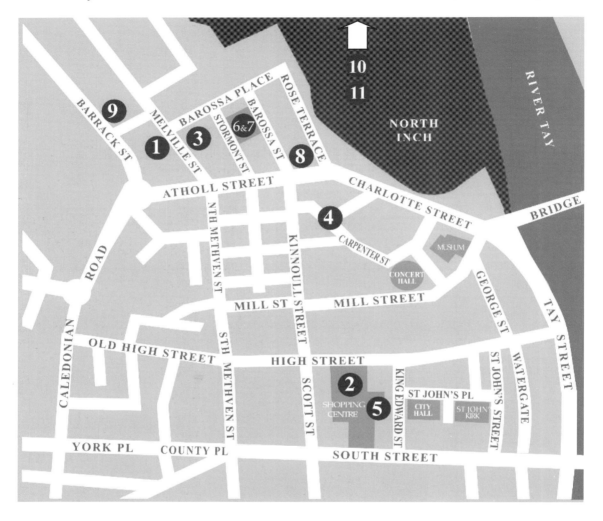

KEY TO MAP

1 St. John's Catholic Church from 1832	6 St. Joseph's Convent (1865-1932?)
2 Meal Vennel	7 St. John's School, Stormont St. (1938-2011)
3 17 Melville Street	8 Corner House Annexe (1941-1967)
4 Carpenter Street	9 Balhousie Annexe (1952-1970)
5 St. John's School, High St. (1860-1938)	10 St. Columba's High School (1967-2009)
	11 St. John's Academy (2009 onwards)

Map by Roben Antoniewicz

Introduction: Before 1832

One of the famous dates in the long history of Perth is Sunday 11th May 1559, the occasion of John Knox's visit to St. John's Kirk . Knox was at the height of his fame as a leader of the Scottish Reformation so his visit attracted a large congregation. He knew how to whip up a crowd and his sermon against the excesses of the Catholic Church was so inspiring and defiant that his enthusiastic audience took matters into their own hands. For two days they rampaged through Perth, destroying church buildings and other property. St. John's Kirk, itself, was vandalised and beyond the town walls, the monasteries of the Grey Friars, the Black Friars and the White Friars were laid waste, their extensive lands confiscated and the monks put to flight.

St. John's Kirk dates from medieval times and its dedication to St. John the Baptist, the fearless cousin of Jesus, gave Perth its 'proper' name, *St. John's Toun of Perth*. After the Reformation, St. John's Kirk was restored and returned to its position as chief church of the city but this time as a Protestant church. The monasteries were not as fortunate. They were neglected and soon vanished for ever, commemorated only by the occasional use of their names in the districts where they once stood – Blackfriars Street, Whitefriars Crescent and Greyfriars Burial Ground. Even the title, *St. John's Toun,* fell into disuse and is now best commemorated in the name of the local football team, *St. Johnstone FC.*

Only a few clung to the old Catholic religion and they had to be secretive for fear of persecution. Three centuries would pass before an influx of poor migrants from Ireland and from the Highlands brought hope of refounding Perth's Catholic community.

Above, a formal group from mid 1950s; below, the cast of 'Carrots', the first full-length musical production, in 1984

Chapter One

A Destitute Parish (1830-1856)

Mr. Mackay's legacy

When James Mackay died in 1884, he left the sum of one hundred and seventy-four pounds, six shillings and eleven pence, most of it from a Scottish Widows insurance policy. He did not know that his real legacy was the school he began for a few poor children fifty-two years earlier and that, almost two centuries later, it would be a one thousand-strong community in a shining new building beside the River Tay.

Mr. Mackay takes charge

James Mackay arrived in Perth in June 1832. He was thirty years old, a Highlander by birth and upbringing who had been working in Edinburgh. His job was a rarity in 1830s Scotland for James Mackay was a Catholic priest.

His first task in Perth was to complete the work begun by his predecessor, Rev. John Geddes who, at the age of twenty five, had died suddenly. John Geddes was the first Catholic priest in Perth since the Reformation. His congregation consisted of 'several hundred destitute Catholics,' yet, despite their poverty, and under his leadership, they started building a church in the new part of Perth, on a site in Melville Street.

When James Mackay arrived, he found the church building project in trouble. Some contractors had failed but shortage of cash was the main reason for delay. Almost immediately, he undertook the fund-raising journey planned by his predecessor to parishes in north and eastern Scotland, a tour which was so successful, financially, that the new church was completed by the end of the year.

The church was named after St. John the Baptist, the fearless cousin of Jesus and Perth's patron saint. It was opened formally on Sunday, 16th December, 1832. Mr. Mackay celebrated solemn High Mass for a packed congregation of parishioners and church dignitaries and the Edinburgh Chapel choir, borrowed for the great occasion, sang Mozart.

Today the Catholic Church of St. John the Baptist still stands in Melville Street but it has been much altered and extended. Mr. Mackay's original construction is described as a

> …plain and substantial building, combining solidity with commodiousness, and simplicity with elegance, situated in one of the most eligible quarters of the town.

It cost £1300 to build.

With the church in place, James Mackay's thoughts turned to the matter of a school.

Mr. Mackay starts a school

There was an education system, of sorts, in Scotland but it was not compulsory and was not provided by the State. Each parish was expected to provide an elementary school and each town to have a grammar school but by the early nineteenth century the system was breaking down due to increasing numbers of children and an inadequate supply of teachers.

The shortage of school places meant that many private schools sprang up to meet the demand for a grounding in the 3Rs. Most were small concerns, catering for a handful of children. Some were successful; others not.

Once James Mackay and his congregation had opened their church, they considered the situation of the children. There was no provision for their education and their parents could not afford the fees charged by Perth Academy and some other establishments. Nor could the St. John's congregation afford to build a school of its own so soon after completing the church. Mr.

Mackay solved the problem by making his church dual purpose and turning it into a part-time school. He became the teacher and gathered 'the poorer children into the chapel…teaching them for four hours every day.' It was the start of the St. John's parish school.

In the following years, Mr. Mackay's church and congregation thrived but the lack of proper accommodation and funding was a continuing problem for the school.

In a neat piece of manoeuvering, Mr. Mackay squeezed some money out of Perth Academy by providing some of its pupils with lodging and extra tuition in his home. But it wasn't enough and his eventual status as the only Catholic priest in Perthshire, brought competing demands from his other parishes in Crieff (17 miles to the west of Perth) and Blairgowrie (16 miles to the north east) to which he travelled on foot.

However, Mr. Mackay did not have the chance to put his school on a more formal basis for in 1846 he was removed from his parish work and sent to a strange new post as chaplain to the Laird of Murthly, Sir William Drummond Stewart.

Drummond Stewart had a colourful past as a military adventurer during the Napoleonic Wars and, later, as a Wild West explorer. After inheriting the Murthly estates he built a typically over-the-top chapel. James Mackay was appointed as chaplain in time for the opening of the chapel, named after St. Anthony the Eremite, on Sunday, 1st November 1846 and thus ended his involvement with education in Perth.

School on the move

Mr. Mackay's successor in Perth was an Irishman, Dr. John McCorry. He led a number of attempts to establish a school. None was permanent but some lasted longer than others.

Dr. McCorry opened his first school in 1848. It was situated in the Seven Star Close, off the High Street, and was in the charge of a Mr. O'Hara. He was succeeded by a Mr. Lafferty 'who taught for a number of years in a small hall at the back of Greig's Close in the High Street'. In this instance a disagreement between parish priest and schoolmaster seems to have hastened the school's closure but soon a Mr. McKeown was teaching sixty-five

Dr. John McCorry was a well-known preacher. The texts of a number of his sermons are still held in the National Library of Scotland in Edinburgh.

children in attic accommodation near the Meal Vennel. This was followed by a class at 17, Melville Street, opposite St. John's Church. Finally there was a sharing of the premises of Lowe's Dancing Academy in Carpenter Street where a Miss Cattanach was teacher.

Two significant events brought the years of nomadic schooling to a close. In 1855, Dr. McCorry received a handsome donation from an anonymous benefactor and used the money to purchase old property behind the High Street and close to the rear of the Meal Vennel. His intention was to demolish the old buildings and, at some unspecified time, to build a school on the site.

The second significant event was the sudden arrival, in 1856, of a new parish priest, the Rev. George Rigg.

Chapter Two

An Ample Supply of Slate Pencils
(1856-1871)

The newcomer

The arrival of a new parish priest at St. John's took everyone by surprise, including the man who had been doing the job for the previous ten years. Dr. McCorry was on a tour of Ireland raising money to build a school and was ignorant of the sudden turn of events in Perth which would deprive him of any further interest in the school.

The move was a surprise, too, for the new priest, Dr. Rigg, who thought he was well-established in Edinburgh. For eighteen years he had been in charge of St. Mary's, an important church behind the east end of Princes Street, which would later become the city's Catholic Cathedral. During that time he grew into a well-known and popular figure in the capital due to his outgoing personality and his committed work for his parishioners. He was interested in education in particular and recently had built St. Mary's School for the children of the parish. It was a notable achievement and showed Dr. Rigg at the peak of his influence and energy. He was also an excellent ambassador for the city's Catholics since many members of local Protestant churches were numbered as his friends, having been attracted by his warm and humorous personality.

Dr. Rigg was also known for his strong views and many people thought that his sudden removal to Perth was due to expressing them once too often. The local church leader – and Dr. Rigg's superior – Bishop Gillis, was losing patience with the priest's opposition to some of his plans, especially his efforts to allocate a city parish to 'incomer' priests of the Jesuit order.

Whatever the truth behind Dr. Rigg's removal from Edinburgh, he began his stay in Perth with his customary whirlwind of activity. He wanted, especially, to establish a parish school and to gain official recognition as a chaplain to Perth Prison. At the time, Perth was the main prison for Scotland but although many of its inmates were Catholics there was no Catholic chaplain. Indeed, the idea was looked upon with such suspicion that Fr. Rigg's early approaches met with opposition and he had to resort to lobbying government officials and ministers.

For the school, success was quicker. The site purchased by Dr. McCorry was cleared and by 1860 St. John's School was built, staffed and open for business. Its situation through the close at 140 High Street placed it firmly amongst the families it was meant to serve. It was set amongst the tenements and builders yards which occupied the area bounded by the High Street, Meal Vennel and South Street – approximately the area now covered by the shops in the St. John's Centre.

The Meal Vennel was largely inhabited by poor Irish migrants who took manual work on the land and on the railways. Later it became known, locally, as the 'Irish Channel,' probably not as a term of affection.

Perth in 1860
By 1860 Perth was thriving. Its population was 24,000 and it was the eighth largest town in Scotland. The railway, whisky and dry cleaning industries were large employers and the families of Bell, Dewar, Pullar and Sandeman were already famous.

St. John's School did not belong to prosperous and confident Perth. It drew its pupils from the city's poorest families. Parents and children lived in single rooms in closes running off the High Street, South Street and the Meal Vennel. They had little furniture, few clothes and were short of food. Parents would have taken whatever low paid work they could find and it would have been menial because many of them would not have been able to read or write.

An item from the *Perthshire Advertiser* illustrates the conditions of the very poor. There was a long period of extreme cold in

February 1860 and under the headline, *Distress of the Poor,* the newspaper reports:

> Forty-one persons, women and ragged children were found at the Dung Depot, grubbing amongst loads of ashes brought from town, for half-burnt cinders to find heat.

An issue from the same period tells of the appearance in Court of John Stewart, a 13 year-old Perth boy, who had stolen a pair of lace-up boots from the shop of McNabs in the High Street. He was sentenced to 20 days in prison. Perhaps he was warmer and better clad in jail.

Some of these children would have attended St. John's but they had more urgent needs than learning to read and count.

St. John's School opens

On the first teaching day in 1860, pupils were welcomed by two teachers, Miss Douglas and Miss Cattanach, both of whom had staffed Dr. McCorry's schools at Melville Street and Lowe's Dancing Academy in Carpenter Street. Miss Douglas was in charge and would teach older pupils while Miss Cattanach taught infants. Dr. Rigg had the title of School Manager as required by government. He would receive official correspondence and be responsible for administering the all-important government grant.

The original St. John's School of 1860 was designed by well-known Perth architect Andrew Heiton Jnr. (1823-1894). Amongst his other works in Perth are the City Chambers, Kinnoull School, the Station Hotel, Rosslyn House and St. Mary's Monastery.

Grants were used by central government to contribute to the funding of schools. In its first year, St. John's received twelve pounds, one shilling and eight pence for apparatus and books. There was also an annual grant of £86/1/0d for other expenses, most notably staff salaries.

'Free' schooling, as we know it, had not yet appeared and it was normal and necessary for church congregations to make financial contributions to their schools. In 1861 St. John's parishioners raised £86/14/1d. This almost matched the amount of the central government grant and placed St. John's parish well ahead of any other church in Perth in the funding of a school.

Contemporary plans show that the school was designed to a layout which reflected the teaching arrangements of the time. Infants and juveniles were separate and each section had its own large schoolroom with access to a smaller room. The roll of the overall school was around two hundred and fifty.

Class sizes were large by modern standards. We know that by 1864 the school's juvenile section had 130 pupils, aged from eight to twelve. They had only one teacher, Miss Cattanach, who was by then head teacher after Miss Douglas's marriage. Miss Cattanach was assisted by three pupil-teachers and one monitress. Next door, was another teacher, Miss Elmes, along with two pupil-teachers and a monitress for a hundred infant children.

The pupil-teacher system was widespread in Britain. It was vital to the staffing of schools and survived until the start of the twentieth century. A teacher like Miss Cattanach, responsible for the learning of 130 eight to twelve-year olds, could not be expected to cope on her own. The supply of qualified teachers was poor so the pupil-teacher system was invented to provide support for the teacher and to allow the class to be broken into smaller teaching groups. Even then the qualified teacher would work with a 'class' of sixty or seventy while the pupil-teachers had smaller numbers.

Pupil-teachers were not adults but senior children, aged from 13 years onwards. They signed up for a form of teaching apprenticeship and, in return, were paid a small salary. The qualified teacher responsible for them also received a special bonus for each 'apprentice'. While working in school the pupil-teachers followed a five-year course to qualify for a *Queen's Scholarship* which paid for two years' further study at a 'normal school', usually Glasgow or Edinburgh, or Liverpool. After successful completion of the final examination, they were awarded a certificate qualifying them as teachers.

The first group of pupil-teachers in St. John's were Mary Bird (5th year – about 18 years of age), Margaret McTavish (4th year) and Jane Lynch (3rd year). The Monitress was Honoria McNamara. She would have been a helper and was not studying to be a qualified teacher.

Pupils were organised in a series of stages known as *Standards*, numbered from Standard I to Standard VI. The aim was for a child to pass one Standard per year from age seven to age twelve although the plan did not always work out as expected, usually because of poor attendance or poor ability. In its early days, the best St. John's pupils were preparing for only Standard IV perhaps reflecting the fact that many children would not have received any regular tuition at a time when schooling was not yet compulsory. The curriculum consisted of:

Catechism, Reading, Writing, Arithmetic, Geography, Grammar and the elements of English History.

Scottish History was not considered worthy of inclusion.

The Right Rev. George Rigg, founder of St. John's School in 1860. The photograph was taken twenty years later when he was Bishop of Dunkeld and residing in Perth.

St. John's was a well-equipped school for the time. Miss Cattanach made a record of the school equipment at April 1864. She wrote that the

Books and Apparatus provided for carrying on school work are: An abundant supply of the Reading Books etc., Log Book, Portfolio and the necessary Registers, class rolls etc. 18 Maps, 3 Large Swinging Slates in frames. Four dozen small slates, 4 boxes for holding Slates. 4 Rostrums for Pupil Teachers. An ample supply of pens, slate pencils etc.

The length of the school day was similar to our own but with slightly different timings. The forenoon session was from 10 to 12.30 and the afternoon from 2 to 4.30. Winter brought an earlier start to the afternoon so that children were home before darkness fell.

The best school in Scotland

By 1864, there were changes afoot for St. John's School. After exercising his charm and powers of persuasion at government level, Dr. Rigg eventually gained recognition as first Catholic chaplain to Perth prison and added it to his work in the parish and the school. He was also responsible, beyond the town, for an area that stretched as far as Crieff in the west and northwards into the settlements that we know today as Highland Perthshire. His legendary energy and stamina were admired while his engaging personality meant that he became as popular in Perthshire as he was in Edinburgh.

Then, as suddenly as he arrived, Dr. Rigg was gone. He was recalled to Edinburgh in 1864. Bishop Gillis had died and his successor, Bishop Strain, wishing to have the talented priest working beside him in the capital, reinstated him at St. Mary's. But it was not the last that Perth or St. John's School would hear of Dr. Rigg.

Miss Cattanach was on the move too. In 1865 she disappeared from the record without explanation. Perhaps she took the marriage route like her predecessor, Miss Douglas.

Before they left, Dr. Rigg and Miss Cattanach had the satisfaction of seeing the school receive a most favourable report from Mr. J. Lynch, Her Majesty's Inspector of Schools (HMI). The Schools…

> continue to present the same evidences of eminent success as justified me in saying that they are the best Schools under my inspection in Scotland.

Who could have asked for a better start?

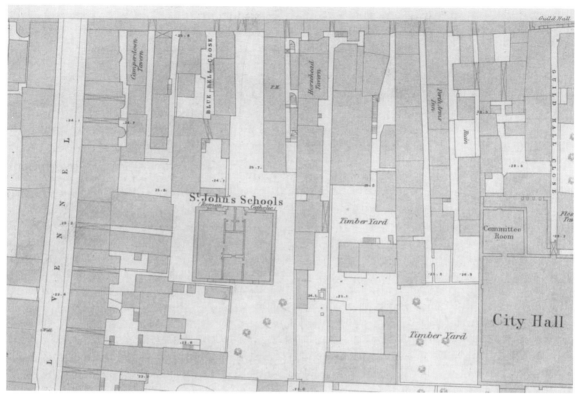

The school settles

Miss Cattanach's departure meant a third head teacher in four years as well as the loss of both the experienced teachers who had established the school.

The new parish priest, Dr. Macpherson, found that Dr. Rigg had left him two extra problems, school staffing and prison visiting. However, he was able to solve both at once by offering the Ursuline Sisters of St. Margaret's Convent in Edinburgh a new settlement in Perth. The offer was conditional on the nuns taking on the task of visiting the Catholic female inmates in Perth Prison of whom there were one hundred and twenty. This was an important task. After Dr. Rigg's efforts in establishing prison access, it could not be allowed to drop upon his departure. The Sisters agreed to take on the prison visiting if their two problems were solved. They had nowhere to stay and, since prison visiting

Detail from an 1860 map of Perth showing the location and outline of the new St. John's School.

High Street is at the top of the map and Meal Vennel to the left. The entrance to the school is through a close from the High Street. The school is surrounded by closes and tenements stretching inwards from the streets. Today most of this area is covered by the St. John's (Shopping) Centre.

The City Hall shown stood from 1845-1907. It was replaced by the present City Hall in 1911.

13

did not pay an income, they had no means of supporting a community in Perth.

Again, Dr. Macpherson had the answers. A suitable property had come on to the market and, with the departure of Miss Cattanach, so had a suitable source of cash. He proposed that the nuns take on the running of the school and use the income to benefit their community. In the longer term, this would bring welcome stability in the supply of school staff.

As for the property, Dr. Macpherson had to look no further than Stormont Street, around the corner from his church. There stood Stormont House once the town house of the Earls of Stormont and latterly a private school. It was for sale and was eminently suitable for a Religious House. So, after approval by the Ursuline Sisters, Dr. Macpherson offered £1850. It was accepted and business was concluded on the 25th March 1865.

On 15th May 1865, a group of six Sisters, led by Mother Mary Angela, took up residence. The name of Stormont House was changed to St. Joseph's Convent. In many ways the site was ideal. It had a substantial formal garden on Stormont Street while the rear of the property, backing on to Barossa Street and twenty feet below the Stormont Street part of the site, was also laid out as a quiet garden with pathways, bushes and trees. Later, when St. Joseph's Convent became the site of the new St. John's School, the garden was concreted over to become the boys' playground. The peace and quiet did not survive the change of use.

Sister Mary Elizabeth took charge of the school. Her own name was Mary Jane Smith and it was used for official education matters. She was assisted by Sister Mary Teresa (Mary Potts). The coming of the Ursuline Sisters began a century-long tradition of nuns in St. John's School. The school association with the Stormont Street site lasted even longer: more than one hundred and forty years, spanning nineteenth, twentieth and twenty-first centuries. Dr. Macpherson's solution to his problems of prison visiting and school staffing, contributed hugely to the St. John's legacy.

Problems appear

When Sister Elizabeth and Sister Teresa arrived at 'the best Schools under my inspection in Scotland,' according to HMI Mr. Lynch, they discovered that no school is perfect and that St. John's had difficulties too.

It appears that poor behaviour, especially from boys, is not just a modern concern. The mid-1860s saw a period of misbehaviour, serious enough to merit entries in the school logbook. It also required the intervention of authorities outside the school: 'Several of the older boys reprimanded by the School Manager for bad conduct.' (6th June 1864). After that came the whistlers: '…Mr. Cumming (assistant priest at St. John's) found fault with one of the boys for whistling in class, a very common fault among them.'(22nd Sept., 1865). Two months later there was a deterioration, perhaps from the same whistlers supported by their friends: 'The boys very noisy and troublesome.' (27th Nov., 1865). The next day brought events to a head: 'Mr. Cumming called and punished several boys for bad behaviour.' (28th Nov. 1865). After that, the Head Teacher records, 'Order in the morning was perfect.' We are not told the nature of the punishment but since the complaint disappears from the logbook, we may assume that Mr. Cumming's firm measures acted as an effective example to the others.

The attendance problem

Soon after its opening, St. John's staff identified a problem which would continue for many years, not just in the nineteenth century but as late as World War II. A May 1864 logbook entry sums up the difficulty succinctly:

> A number of children preparing to pass under Standard I not making any progress. Cause – the irregularity of their attendance.

On many occasions children's attendance was poor and, sometimes, the head teacher recorded attendances lower than seventy per cent. (Today, ninety-five per cent and above would be expected.) Both school staff and inspectors blamed poor attendance for the slow progress made by many children.

In the 1860s, school attendance was not yet compulsory. Amongst the poor there was no tradition of regular school attendance nor was it part of parents' thinking. Their prime concern was to earn enough money to survive, so employment and wage earning were the family's main priorities. At the age of eleven or twelve a boy was expected to find a job to contribute to his family's finances and when he did, he left school immediately. The logbook records some details:

> Several boys and girls…leaving School to go to trades their ages varying from 11 to 14 years. (20th April 1864)

The phrase 'widespread illness' often appeared to explain absence. It covered conditions which we still suffer, like influenza as well as other acute ailments, now rare to us, such as diphtheria and scarlet fever. Typhoid, too, affected Perth, notably killing fifteen people in the year before St. John's School opened. 'Wet weather' caused absence too. A trivial excuse to the modern eye, perhaps, but in 1860 poor children did not have special clothing to protect them from heavy rain, they lacked adequate footwear and had no healthy means of drying out either.

High absences were recorded on special occasions such as Market Day, or a 'fair' like *St. Luke's* or *Little Dunning*. There were six fairs each year. *Little Dunning* was held on the third Friday in October and drew visitors from far and wide. These *hiring fairs* or *feeing markets* took place in towns and large villages and were where casual labourers found agricultural employment for the coming six months. One writer tells us how, 'All the domestic and farm servants claim the right of attending these *feeing markets* as a holiday.' Soon, Perth High Street was crowded with people and cattle enjoying their special day bartering, buying, selling and arranging new jobs. The successful celebrated and the disappointed drowned their sorrows. Whichever way, the town became host to a drunken rabble as the day wore on. With all this happening outside the school's close, successive Head Teachers found it wise to allow pupils to leave early on a *fair* day.

Other regular occasions also encouraged poor attendance. Harvest prevented many children returning to school in September after the summer break as they went *tattie howkin* with their parents. And each May comes the entry,

> School unusually thin. Great numbers of the children leaving town with their parents to go to the woods to peel the oak and are likely to be absent for a month or six weeks.

Peeling the oak provided employment, each Spring, as whole families migrated to the oak woods which surrounded Perth. The leather industry, especially the making of gloves, was important to Perth and the bark of the oak tree was essential for tanning animal hides. Today the oak woods have disappeared – partly because of the bark stripping – and are remembered only in place names such as *Oak-bank* and the *Burgh-muir*.

The Head Teacher's concern about attendance was not just because of the breaks in children's learning. Some of the school's funding came from the government and the level of the grant depended on children's attendance. However, most 1860s parents of St. John's had more important things to consider. Families depended on parents and children taking paid employment whenever they could. Schooling was a luxury compared to survival.

There were other concerns too. Inspectors were still enthusiastic in their reports but what was to be a familiar reservation began to make regular appearances. May 1867 saw the issue raised quietly: '…the instruction, *except in the arithmetic and writing to the Third Standard,* is very satisfactory.' A year later the criticism is more obvious: 'The failures in Arithmetic, especially in the Second Standard, are more numerous than they should be but in other respects very creditable progress has been made.' By May 1869 weaknesses in arithmetic are widespread: 'The failures in Arithmetic are still more numerous than they ought to be, the school in other respects makes creditable progress.'

Ten years on

As the school approached its tenth birthday in 1870, there was an event which could have brought it to a premature end. On a Tuesday evening in February, a passer by noticed smoke coming from the school. His quick thinking and the prompt arrival of the police saved the building from serious damage. The *Perthshire Courier* reported,

> In one of the classrooms a portion of flooring in front of the fireplace had become ignited probably by the falling of a burning coal on it. There was no damage beyond the burning of a few feet of the flooring, a small proportion of the children's gallery and one of the doors of the room.

With conflagration avoided and despite other problems surfacing, the first decade of St. John's School was remarkably successful. Its name was established in the town and it benefited from the foresight of Dr. McCorry and the energy of Dr. Rigg in providing purpose-built accommodation in the heart of its community. The Ursuline Sisters brought settled staffing, the roll was healthy and – with the exception of arithmetic – most pupils were making good progress. Not bad for a school in a poor area which previously had led an uncertain existence, relying on nomadic teachers and temporary accommodation. The slate pencils, noted on Miss Cattanach's list, had been well used.

But the silver lining had a cloud. Shortly after St. John's tenth anniversary, the government presented its *Education (Scotland) Act* of 1872. The Act was supposed to benefit all schoolchildren but it raised serious questions about the future of St. John's.

Chapter Three

Payment by Results (1872-1901)

Government takes over

By 1872, the developments which would make our modern world were well underway. In Britain, Charles Darwin was explaining his theories; in Germany, Gotlieb Daimler was experimenting with the internal combustion engine and a Scotsman, Alexander Graham Bell, arrived in America. In France, Jules Verne, writer of science fiction which became fact, had just published *Twenty Thousand Leagues Under the Sea*. In Scotland the foundation of a modern education system was put in place.

Time was running out for the hotch-potch of schools run by churches, groups and private individuals. Costs were already rising and when the government announced that it planned to make school attendance compulsory for all five to thirteen year-olds, schools knew that their budgets could not pay for an expansion of accommodation and an increase in teachers. The government saw its chance and offered to take over the schools. Most owners handed them over quickly, especially the Church of Scotland and the Free Church who, between them, ran the greatest number of schools.

The government's offer was part of a plan to establish a state education system to ensure that all children could read, write and count.

So, where did St. John's fit in to the government's new education system? Not at all, is the answer. It did not join in.

Not that St. John's, itself, should shoulder any responsibility. The decision was made by Scotland's Catholic church leaders. They decreed that Catholic schools would not take part and, therefore, would not avail themselves of the government's cash. The Reformation, three hundred years before, cast a long shadow and Catholics felt safest within communities of other Catholics. They had struggled to build and fund their own schools and felt they would lose their identity if they became part of a national system. By rejecting it, however, they ensured that they would keep on struggling.

This decision was to cause many problems for St. John's. There would be some money from government but for the major expenses of teachers' salaries and maintenance of buildings, the school was on its own.

The 1872 Act contained some of the most influential education legislation in Scotland's history and the shake-up meant that many schools disappeared overnight. St. John's survived because it was not part of the new national system but the Act was a serious threat to its future.

An old friend returns

A few years after the Education Act, there was an important event in the life of the Catholic Church in Scotland. Since the Reformation, the Vatican had treated Scotland as a missionary country and the British government had not recognised the leaders of Scotland's Catholics. However, this all changed with the nineteenth century growth in numbers and parishes which meant that in 1878 the Catholics of Scotland regained their full status with both Rome and Westminster.

The Pope, Leo XIII, restored the full hierarchy of bishops. New diocese were formed, using the ancient titles where possible, and a number of senior priests were appointed as bishops to lead them. St. John's parish in Perth was to be in the ancient Diocese of Dunkeld. And who should be the first Bishop of Dunkeld? None other than Dr. George Rigg, parish priest of St. John's from 1856-1864, during his temporary exile from Edinburgh, and builder of St. John's School.

The new bishop was consecrated in Rome on 26th May 1878. On his return to Scotland, his first task was to choose his place of residence which would then become principal town of the dio-

cese. Dundee had a strong claim as the largest centre of population but the Bishop chose Perth, which he knew already, and took up residence at St. John's once again. His first visit was to the school he built eighteen years before and throughout his nine years as bishop, the school logbook records his continuing interest in the school and its pupils, sometimes visiting on three or four days each week.

This photograph from the 1880s shows the community of Ursuline Sisters outside Stormont House, later the site of St. John's School. Some of the nuns were teachers in St. John's School then situated behind the High Street.

Bishop Rigg's work in Perth, and in the diocese of Dunkeld, continued until his death, after months of illness, on Tuesday 18th January 1887. The *Scotsman* newspaper reported the tributes paid to him at a service in Edinburgh and at his Requiem Mass in Perth on 21st January. St. John's Church 'was crowded to overflowing' for the ceremonies led by Archbishop Eyre of Glasgow.

The report describes the scene.

Surrounding and covering the coffin were wreaths of flowers and imortelles sent by friends and also vases of cut flowers and pots of heath; and in the coffin were laid the mitre and crosier of the deceased, and the gold chalice presented to him by the Perth Roman Catholics when he left for Edinburgh in 1865.

When he was parish priest in Perth, the bishop built a Lady Chapel behind St. John's Church. It was his favourite place and after the Requiem Mass, the priests of the diocese laid him to rest there in a specially built vault sunk into the floor.

Payment by results

The 1872 Education Act took a new approach to the funding of schools. As a way of raising standards, schools would receive funding depending on the numbers of children they managed to get through the curriculum. A menu of subjects had to be constructed and payments matched against them and there were inspectors to check that the process was working. The whole system was known as *Payment by Results*.

In the school year 1881-1882, the following payments were made to schools whose children qualified.

Grants per pupil for average attendance, music, order and discipline – 6 shillings each.

For infants presented – 8 shillings each

Passes in Reading, Writing and Arithmetic – 3 shillings each (no grant for anyone passing in only one of the subjects).

Classes in Grammar and Intelligence, Geography and History – 4 shillings

Teachers who taught drawing obtained the science and art grant

Problems grow for Catholic schools

The decision by the Catholic Church to turn down the invitation to join the national system of schools in 1872 had serious consequences for Catholic schools which then had to survive without financial help from the government or the new local School Boards. This meant that the church had to find the money to pay its teachers and to maintain its buildings and since, in Scotland, most of its parishoners were poor, the finding of money became a serious burden.

Teachers' salaries made up the bulk of a school's expenditure even although Catholic teachers were paid less than teachers in Board schools. The average Catholic school staff costs for 1910 are given with the average Board school salaries in brackets: Principal masters £148 (£189); principal mistresses £94 (£95); assistant masters £94 (£136); assistant mistresses £73 (£81). Male teachers are paid more than female and, at each level, the Catholic school salary is lower; in the case of male teachers, substantially lower.

To have any chance of survival, Catholic schools had to keep staffing costs as low as possible. There were several ways of achieving this. First was not to employ male teachers. Second was to hand a school over to an order of nuns who could be paid a pittance. Third was to rely heavily on pupil-teachers who earned much less than a qualified teacher. All three steps towards cost restriction were employed in St. John's. (The use of pupil-teachers continued in Catholic schools long after it ended in Board schools.)

There was also concern about the quality of some of the teachers employed in Catholic schools. At the start of the twentieth century, Catholic schools would only employ Catholics, usually only women prepared to work for a lower rate of pay, and a high number of cheap pupil-teachers. If you set criteria which exclude a high proportion of the country's teachers, it is possible that your restricted choice may not always give you the best.

To make matters worse, the pace of change in education increased and Catholic schools found themselves trying to keep up with developments in the government-funded Board schools.

Nationally, after 1872, there was a steady growth in the number of women qualifying to teach and the increased teacher supply meant that the size of classes could be reduced. Smaller classes would require smaller rooms, with the old schoolrooms which could hold more than one hundred children, now redundant. Buildings had to be altered, usually by partitioning the large spaces, to make a larger number of smaller rooms.

In 1901, the school leaving-age was raised to 14 and with an extra year group in school, there was a further demand for accommodation. Then there was the expanding curriculum with facilities required for sewing, drill and singing. More teachers and better facilities all had to be paid for. For Catholic schools, it meant more fund-raising; like the two-day bazaar held by St. John's parish in the (old) City Hall in 1903. More than £900 was raised for the school, an astonishing sum by any standard.

During this period, the role of the parish priest was vital to the survival of St. John's school. He was the official Manager who answered directly to the Bishop and to the Scotch Education Department, (as it was called) but, above all, it was his efforts that kept the school alive. He had to find money, or raise it from his parishioners, to pay teachers. That is, if he could find properly qualified teachers in sufficient numbers, a thankless task which could involve scouring the whole of Britain. He also had to raise money for the maintenance of the school building and pay for the extensions that it required over the years. Inspectors acknowledged such efforts in 1904:

> The Managers have materially improved the conditions of school work by adding two classrooms and by remedying two defects in ventilation.

St. John's School owes a great debt to the parish priests of the 1872 – 1918 period: Revvs. William Smith, Joseph Holder, William Geddes and Thomas Walsh and Canons John Turner and Michael Lavelle.

"Considering the peculiar circumstances of the school…"

The Payment by Results regime required that children were tested each year by Her Majesty's Inspectors (HMI) who visited the school and made a written report. These reports are still available and give a feel of the school's triumphs and difficulties during that time. For most of the period the HMI visiting St. John's was Mr. Alex Walker who built up a detailed knowledge of the school, its pupils and staff.

It's now that we hear regularly about the serious problems which faced St. John's. The arithmetic weaknesses, already identified, continue but there is a parade of worrying phrases which repeat through the years. The first inspection of the new regime states: *'Considering the class of children and their very irregular attendance,* the elementary work is well done.' (May 1873) In the following years we find: *'…considering the class of children…'* (Nov. 1875) *'…considering the class most of them belong to.'* (Dec. 1878) *'Considering the class of children and the irregularity of attendance,* the results of the examination are very creditable.' (Jan. 1881) *'…considering the peculiar circumstances of the school…'* (Dec. 1882) *'…taking into account the circumstances of the children,* the progress made in the usual subjects of instruction is very creditable.' (Dec. 1896). In his November 1876 report, Mr. Walker spells out the *peculiar circumstances*:

Shuttlefield Close, one of the many poor parts of Perth. The photo was taken in 1881 as it was being demolished to make way for the building of Scott Street. It is likely that some of St. John's pupils came from this area.

> The school labours under peculiar disadvantages from the class of children, the number of half-timers and irregular attendance.

He is still writing in this way in his final report, more than twenty years later, when he concludes:

> Altogether highly creditable work has been done *in difficult circumstances*. (January 1898)

HMI Mr. Walker is fair in his judgments and regularly gives credit to the efforts of teachers. He acknowledges difficulties in attainment.

> The school, under much disadvantage from irregular attendance, continues to be ably and successfully taught. (December 1885)

He is sympathetic to the children also and does not blame them for poor achievement in their learning.

> Very good order is maintained and taking into account the circumstances of the children, the progress made in the usual subjects of instruction is very creditable. (December 1896)

Usually the work of younger classes meets the Inspector's approval while problems are more obvious in older classes. Mr. Walker's comments in 1876 contain a serious compliment:

> The work of the First and Second Standards was very well done and will compare favourably with that of any other school in the town.

A few years later, in 1881, the compliment extends further,

> In the first four Standards all the work is exceedingly well done.

Throughout this period Arithmetic proves to be a consistent problem while there are regular problems with Grammar and Spelling:

The Grammar was poor except in the fourth Standard and the Arithmetic of all above the second Standard was somewhat defective! (1877) (or) ...there are too many failures in Arithmetic. (1884)

In 1896 the inspector manages to criticise more than ever:

...Spelling in the third, Composition in the fifth and Arithmetic in the sixth are weak, Reading is throughout hurried and stumbling, and none of the classes examined showed a really intelligent grasp of Grammar. The style of Writing is also somewhat careless.

But the next report shows the difference a year can make:

Written results in Arithmetic are about excellent and mental Arithmetic has received some attention. Spelling in all the class, except the third, is weaker. The Reading Books are, as a rule, well known, but the general style of reading is still too hurried and defective in phrasing. As regards class subjects, knowledge of Geography has

This 1901 photo shows the junction of Kinnoull Street with Atholl Street and Barossa Street. Look to the large part of open land on the left of Barossa Street. This was the grounds of St. Joseph's Convent with gardens sloping from Stormont Street to Barossa Street. In the mid-1930s the convent was demolished and the site used for the new St. John's School. The photo appears to have been taken from the top of Pullar's chimney, a vantage point demolished in 1980.

greatly improved, particularly in the third and fourth but Grammar is still very weak in the fifth and accurate expression in the lower classes requires cultivation. Singing, sewing and drill are all very satisfactory. Altogether highly creditable work has been done in difficult circumstances.

By the final decade of the nineteenth century, the curriculum was expanding and becoming more adventurous, especially for older children. Geography and History appeared and then, as teachers became available, so did singing, sewing and drill. Drill showed its military origins in the title of the instructor, Sergeant Magee.

Illness continued to affect school attendance seriously. In December 1899, Dr. Stuart ordered St. John's to close early for Christmas because of an epidemic of measles. By the time it reopened in January, influenza was widespread and in February attendance was affected by storms and severe weather as well as the continuing flu. It was March before the head could report, 'Attendance much improved.'

Not everyone's attendance was disappointing. In November 1899, the school's manager and parish priest, Canon John Turner, made presentations to children with good attendance. Those who had not been absent during the year received silver badges and gold crosses and there was one boy who had not missed school in four years. He was awarded a silver watch which must have been an unusual and expensive gift for a child. We are not told if any of the recipients later fell foul of that winter's severe attacks of measles or flu.

Mr. Mackay goes south

After his groundbreaking work in the schooling of poor children in Perth, James Mackay spent some years in what we now call Highland Perthshire. He was chaplain at the Murthly estate and, at the same time, he looked after the Catholic community in Blairgowrie. Later, when Blairgowrie had its own priest, he added Tullimet and Grandtully to his responsibilities.

In 1862, two years after Rev. George Rigg opened the first permanent St. John's School, Mr. Mackay was on the road south and out of Scotland. He seems to have been a nomad for a time, perhaps staying in Walsall and then in 1864, turning up in Leicestershire at Mount St. Bernard's Abbey, a monastery of Cistercian monks.

He settled at Mount St. Bernard's and became the parish priest, a position which could not be filled by a monk as it would have conflicted with his duty to the monastery community. James Mackay served the parishioners at Mount St. Bernard's and in the surrounding country for another twenty-two years. He died at Mount St. Bernard's on 19th April 1884 at the age of eighty-two. Fifty years had passed since he took the first steps in giving an education to some of Perth's poorest children.

Long lost Victorian photos?

No - just some modern attempts by St. John's pupils to imagine part of Victorian life. In any case, they look far too clean and healthy for Victorian urchins.

Top photos are from 1988 and, right, 'Please Sir, may I have some more?' is from the 1987 production of 'Oliver!'

Chapter Four

Problems Galore (1901-1937)

The wide world of 1901

The twentieth century began with the death in January 1901 of the ninety year-old Queen Victoria. For almost everyone in Britain, Victoria was the only monarch they had known. She was succeeded by her son who reigned as King Edward VII. In Perth he would be remembered by King Edward Street the access road for the new city hall.

Britain's war against the South African Boers was coming to an end although it would be another year before fighting ceased. In America, there was a change of leader with the death of President McKinley as the result of an assassin's bullet and the succession of the Vice President, Theodore (Teddy) Roosevelt. We remember President Roosevelt best for giving his name to the Teddy Bear.

Inventions which are commonplace today were at crucial phases in their development. Marconi transmitted the first radio signals across the Atlantic from Britain to Canada, instant coffee was invented and King C. Gillette started production of the *Gillette Safety Razor*.

St. John's school building at 1902

In 1902, the church submitted plans for an additional two classrooms at St. John's. The plans have survived in the Council Archives and show the school's growth since 1860. Added buildings and extensions meant it had become the largest occupant of the area bounded by High Street, South Street and Meal Vennel yet it was well hidden with no direct view from the main streets.

Class photograph from 1920.

Access continued to be from the close at 140 High Street where pupils had to pass the conveniently placed Stratton's Confectioners at number 138. There was another entry through a close in the Meal Vennel.

The two large Victorian schoolrooms of the original building were subdivided into four classrooms. The most significant change was the addition of a long building at the rear of the site containing five classrooms and an office. One classroom was designated for science and the office was labelled 'Headmaster,' despite St. John's always having a headmistress.

Each classroom was heated by a coal fire and it was the duty of the janitor to ensure that fires were cleaned out and working throughout the day. In the playground, he had the necessary coal shed.

While the headmistress had an office, with coal fire, there were no facilities for staff other than lavatories. Nor is there any gym accommodation since 'drill' would have been conducted in the playground. Pupils' lavatories were outside too and, follow-

Class photograph from 1904. This would be around the time that Dr. Stuart was drawing attention to the 'poor physiques' of children at St. John's. The nun may be Sister Winifrede who was headmistress between 1910 and 1918

ing the Victorian tradition, girls and boys had separate playgrounds, a practice which would continue to Stormont Street and survive until the present day.

The 1902 plans show two additional classrooms being added to the original block so that forty years after it opened, St. John's had grown to eleven classrooms. (Another two would be added in the early 1930s.)

Dr. Stuart makes a survey

School inspectors commented, regularly, on the difficulties many St. John's pupils suffered because of illness and poverty and by the turn of the century the British government found that, across the country, many of the working class boys applying to join the army were unfit for service due to poor health. The resulting campaign to improve children's health led to Perth's medical officer, Dr. Charles Stuart, examining all the schoolchildren in the city. His report drew attention to St. John's.

> As regards the physique of the [pupils in] individual schools, those in the outskirts of the town – Craigie, Kinnoull and Cherrybank – easily take premier place…while at the other end of the table are those schools situated in congested parts of the town, such as Central (very bad) and St. John's.

Dr. Stuart stated that it was not schools which made the differences in children's growth:

> These schools [St. John's and Central] as regards buildings and equipment, are in every way as good as the other schools.

The causes of children's poor physiques were to be found at home.

> They have less fresh air, and in too many cases their food is inferior, and their defects are neglected.

Hard words, perhaps, but they confirmed the difficulties school inspectors had been highlighting for four decades.

Change in the air
The early decades of the twentieth century saw two important developments in the organisation of Scottish education both of which are still with us. World War I may have raged between 1914 and 1918 but government found time to push the idea of compulsory state education which it almost achieved with the 1872 Act.

The Catholic Church refused to join the 1872 system and set out on more than forty years of trying to sustain its own schools, St. John's amongst them.

For St. John's, the first decade of the twentieth century was a particularly troubling time. Maintenance was required on the forty year-old building as well as altering and extending it to cope with new subjects and smaller classes.

Above, class photograph from 1922.

Staffing was a problem

Of course, smaller classes meant more teachers and with teachers in Catholic schools paid substantially less than Board School teachers, schools like St. John's had difficulty in attracting staff. In Glasgow in 1917 a male assistant teacher in a Catholic school was paid just over £94 in a year while his equivalent in a Board school earned £154 and twelve shillings (£154/12/-).

Since the early days of St. John's, pupil-teachers had been used; they were older pupils who taught younger pupils under the supervision of a qualified teacher. This was not unusual. All schools did it. However, when starting the state system in 1872, the government soon replaced pupil-teachers with properly qualified teachers. The Catholic Church did not carry out this replacement in its schools. Indeed as late as 1906 we find the Bishop of Dunkeld, Bishop Macfarlane, stating that, 'Every school must take on pupil teachers.' Pupil teachers were cheaper but they also concealed the poor supply of qualified Catholic teachers who would work for low pay.

Above, the St. John's percussion band from around the mid 1920s. Below, a South Street vennel from 1934. Some children who lived there would have attended St. John's School.

A St. John's incident illustrates the problem. In 1904 two teachers – Miss Agnew and Miss Gethin – asked for an increase in salary but the school manager (the parish priest) refused. The teachers resigned. The school manager, Canon Lavelle, had difficulty in replacing them. He wrote that he, 'applied to Training Colleges and other centres as well as advertised. For some time (my) efforts were unsuccessful.' The government wouldn't recognise one lady that he proposed because she was unqualified and when he did find someone, she was not available for another six weeks.

Then, the school inspector questioned the qualifications of some other staff including one of the nuns. As far as he could tell they were unqualified and since no opposing argument was presented, we can assume he was right. So, with few staff and some of them unqualified at that, the headmistress ended up teaching more than sixty pupils each day for two months.

To complicate matters further, there was a financial penalty for employing unqualified and unapproved staff so, in this case, St. John's suffered a reduction in its annual grant for 'insufficiency of staff throughout the year…'

The log book entry about staffing difficulties appeared only after pressure from inspectors. It is likely that the problems were not confined to one year only but were a running sore throughout this period when Catholic schools were having to fund themselves. As for Miss Agnew and Miss Gethins, probably they did not teach in a Catholic school again.

Class photograph from around 1920, including some examples of the 'Eton collar', smart boys' wear of the period. The girls' alternative is the hair ribbon.

The 1918 Education Act

The upkeep of buildings, payment of teachers, and provision of the extra accommodation required by an expanding curriculum, was more than could be financed by sales of work and Sunday collections, especially in a country where most parishes were poor. Church leaders were split. Some foresaw that joining the state system would be necessary for survival while others had reservations.

The government was concerned about the poor staffing of Catholic schools and the lower attainment of their pupils. This fuelled its push for the inclusion of Catholic schools in the state system and politicians believed that until this happened, they would not achieve a good level of education for all children.

Negotiations between government and the Catholic Church began in 1905. Progress was so slow that it took until 1918 to bring in legislation and even then some of the Church's leaders were opposed to giving up their schools. So desperate was the government to run Scotland's Catholic schools that it offered the church the incentive, or bribe, of a veto on the appointment of teachers. To this day, teachers appointed to work in a Catholic school have to be approved by the church, not in terms of their academic qualifications and experience but in their standing as Catholics.

However, it was the end of priests' day-to-day involvement in running Catholic schools. Many priests had worked hard to establish Catholic schools and keep them going but the education authority was now the manager and – along with government – the provider of finance and setter of policy.

The First World War

The supposed 'War to end all wars' lasted from August 1914 to November 1918. It doesn't feature in the school records but it would have had a direct effect on the families of St. John's pupils, many of whom would have had older brothers fighting in the trenches of the Western Front in Belgium and France. Some of those brothers were killed.

In their minutes, Perth School Board listed former pupils of Perth schools who lost their lives fighting 'for King and Country.' The St. John's names are published in Appendix 4 of this book.

The photograph, below, of the St. John's Scouts probably is related to the church rather than the school since some of the boys are of working age. It is dated 1909 but may be a little later since Baden Powell founded the Scout movement only in 1907.

Many of the boys will have fought and died in the First World War, 1914-18.

A new head

The new era ushered in by the 1918 Education Act was accompanied by the appointment, in 1924, of St. John's first male head, Mr. James Begg. It ended sixty-four continuous years of female heads, most of whom were members of a religious order, and began eighty years of male heads.

No doubt the equalising of pay between teachers in Catholic schools and those in local authority schools meant that more women and men could afford to teach in Catholic schools and, eventually, offer themselves as head teachers. Nor did the male head mean the end of nuns, some of whom remained on the staff until as late as the 1970s.

Wretched accommodation

Dr. Stuart's successor as school medical officer, Dr. Mary Macdonald, continued his crusade against poverty when she examined school buildings. In 1918 she wrote to the Perth School Board,

Class photograph from late 1920s showing, beyond the wall, the City Hall. Today, this is the entrance from King Edward Street to the Saint John's shopping centre.

The man in the back row is Mr. Begg, headmaster from 1924. The nun's head dress tells us she is a Sister of Charity, the order which replaced the Ursuline Sisters.

> The (outside) lavatories at St. John's RC School have become so unhealthy that I have made arrangements for the renewal of the whole of the woodwork and the urinal.

At least St. John's was in good company with its lavatorial problems because Dr. Macdonald added:

> On the boys' side of the Academy, there is room for considerable improvement.

Two years later Dr. Macdonald returned to her theme, branding the St. John's gym facilities as 'unfit for use.'

By the 1930s the concerns about lavatories and gym had grown into a serious concern about the whole St. John's building with inspectors drawing attention to the poor state of the school building they had once called excellent.

The inspectors' campaign started with a flurry of activity. On 16th February 1932, the headmaster records,

> Mr. Kerr HMI called to make a report on buildings.

Class photograph from 1920.

Class photograph from 1920. 'Eton collars' and hair ribbons in evidence again.

Two days later,

> Dr. Smith HM Chief Inspector for Scotland visited school for purpose of reporting on buildings.

It seems that Dr. Smith, having received an extreme report from Mr. Kerr, had to see for himself. By 22nd February, the news had spread further and,

> Mr. Hodge, Chairman of the Education Committee of the County Council, visited school today.

We can guess why.

A year later, the inspectors left no doubt about their views with remarks which could not have been more damning:

> …the accommodation is wretched and pupils and teachers are seriously handicapped by the depressing and miserable conditions in which they have to work.

Class photograph from around 1934. Headmaster, Mr. James Begg, is at the far right of the back row.

This was not just peeling paint but complete condemnation.

But it was not only the school. The housing in the Meal Vennel area was under attack too. The council started to talk about 'slum clearance' and drew up plans for a replacement development of modern dwellings and well-appointed gardens. However, the Second World War delayed the Meal Vennel demolition until 1955.

There was no future, either, for St. John's School in the town centre so the education authority decided to build a new school on the site in Stormont Street where St. Joseph's convent, owned by the church, stood empty.

The name's the same...

But look what happened to the site

St. John's School to St. John's Square to St. John's Centre

Look over the wall

The photograph shows the great and the good of Perth gathered for the opening of the memorial to King Edward VII in 1913. Top hats were the order of the day but there's a special interest in looking beyond the foreground.

The wall behind the Mercat Cross is the boundary of the original St. John's School and this photograph gives the best impression of the school at that time.

By this date, the school ground was tightly packed with the buildings which were added piecemeal as it grew. In the centre right, with raised skylights, is Dr. Rigg's original school. Running from the centre backwards is the substantial late Victorian addition. Two more classrooms were added in 1902 and another two in the early 1930s. By then the site was congested.

For a view from the school side of the wall, see the photograph on page 39.

When the Rev. George Rigg built St. John's School in 1860, it was surrounded by closes and run-down housing and poor people were packed into the area.

By the start of the twentieth century, the school found itself on the edge of a posh new development as the council decided to build a city hall that would reflect their grand ambitions for Perth.

Some of the slum property was demolished and the (present) City Hall was built between 1909 and 1914. King Edward Street was constructed for access and when the King died, the councillors decided to build a memorial to him in the form of a new Mercat Cross.

St. John's Square (1961-1985) is at the top and its successor, St. John's Centre, is below. The Mercat Cross is the only landmark which links both photos to the 1913 photo on the previous page. Using the Mercat Cross as a reference, it's easy to see, where the original St. John's School stood. The photos, here, also suggest that the St. John's Square clock survived onto the front of the St. John's Centre.

Redeveloping the Meal Vennel

With the opening of the new school in Stormont Street in 1938, the original St. John's lived on in a twilight existence of parish activities, wedding receptions, training for wartime emergencies and Perth Fire Brigade whose Station was nearby in King Edward Street.

The Council's plans to redevelop the Meal Vennel area had been delayed because of the war but, eventually, in 1955, all the slum properties and the original St. John's School were demolished.

An architectural competition

The Council held a competition for the redevelopment of the area. It was won by a firm of Glasgow architects. Their concept of a mix of modern shopping and residential properties was named St. John's Square and was opened in 1961. But it was not a success and didn't last long. St. John's Square was demolished in 1985.

Let's try again

In 1988 St. John's Square was replaced by an indoor shopping area known as the St. John's Centre. It covered a slightly larger area and involved the disappearance of the ancient Meal Vennel.

Chapter Five

This Magnificent School (1938)

The wide world of 1938

Many of the 'firsts' from 1938 are still with us. In Dundee, D.C. Thomson published the first edition of the *Beano* complete with free 'whoopee mask' while Hungarian Laszlo Biro patented his invention of the ballpoint pen. Scotland celebrated another example of its industrial might when the liner, *Queen Elizabeth* was launched by the Queen (later Queen Elizabeth, the Queen Mother) at John Brown's shipyard in Clydebank and Glasgow welcomed the world to its Empire Exhibition at Bellahouston Park.

Glenn Miller and his Band had a big hit with *Moonlight Serenade* while cinemagoers enjoyed a clutch of films which would become famous. There was *Angels with Dirty Faces* starring James Cagney; *The Lady Vanishes* directed by Alfred Hitchcock; Walt Disney's *Snow White and the Seven Dwarfs* and Errol Flynn in *The Adventures of Robin Hood*. In football, Italy, the holders, won the World Cup beating Hungary 4-2 in Paris while Celtic were Scottish League Champions. The Scottish Cup was won by East Fife in a 4-2 victory over Kilmarnock in front of a Hampden crowd of ninety-two thousand.

Most importantly, this was the year when Europe found itself close to war. The German Chancellor, Adolph Hitler, had already annexed Austria and now set out his plans to take over the Sudetenland, part of Czechoslovakia. British Prime Minister, Neville Chamberlain, along with other European leaders met Hitler in Munich at the end of September in the hope of 'appeasing' him. They agreed not to oppose his capture of the Sudetenland if he would halt his annexation of other lands.

In 1938, Perth had four cinemas: the Alhambra in Kinnoull Street; the King's Cinema in South Methven Street; the Cinerama in Victoria Street and the Playhouse in Murray Street. Only the Playhouse remains.

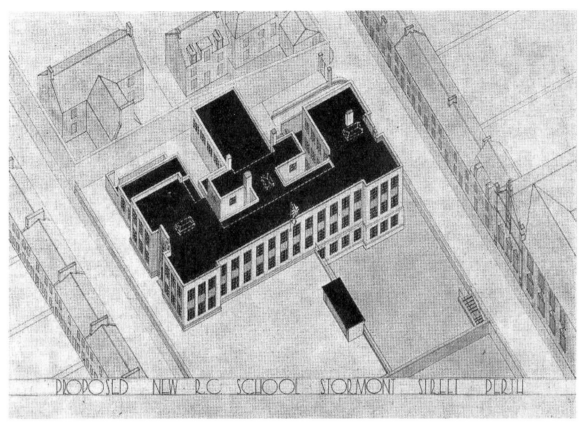

An architect's drawing from 1936 of the proposed new St. John's. Stormont Street is to the left and Barossa Street to the right. The viewpoint from above shows how well the building fits on to a difficult stepped site with two floors at the front and three floors at the rear.

Hitler agreed and, amidst celebrations, Chamberlain returned home waving the paper that Hitler had signed, declaring that it guaranteed 'peace in our time'. However, Hitler placed less weight on the paper than Chamberlain and one year later, after Hitler's invasion of Poland, Chamberlain was forced to declare war on Germany.

The new St. John's was born into an eventful time.

The 'magnificent school' opens

The new St. John's School in Stormont Street opened in 1938 on 24th June, the feast day of the school's patron, St. John the Baptist.

The day was fine and, in the afternoon, a large number of local dignitaries gathered in the Stormont Street playground to

witness the opening of Perth's newest building. The opening ceremony was conducted by Monsignor Turner, Vicar General of the Diocese of Dunkeld and once an assistant priest in St. John's Parish.

The invited guests represented the communities connected with the school. Various council officials attended including the Director of Education, Dr. Dawson, the County Clerk, Mr. Marshall and the Convenor of the County Council, Mr. Henderson. Members of the Education Committee and the Perth School Management Committee turned out as did representatives of the various building contractors. Invitations were also accepted by the heads of other Perth schools such as Balhousie Boys', Southern District (in Nelson Street and now demolished) and Western District (now Craigie School).

The Catholic Church was represented by a number of priests, including the Parish Priest, Canon McDaniel, and a message of

Monsignor Turner at the front door as he opens, officially, the new St. John's School. He is accompanied by Mr. A. W. Allison , architect, (far left) and Dr. R. Stirling, Chairman of the Perth School Management Committee.

47

Around this time St. John's had a school motto, according to a contemporary presentation certificate. In Latin it was 'Ut Probetis Potiora' and comes from St. Paul's First Epistle to the Phillipians.

The English translation, 'To value the better things,' is apt for any educational establishment.

Today 'Ut Probetis Potiora' is the motto of the Franciscan university in Milwaukee, Wisconsin, USA.

appreciation was sent by the leader of the Diocese of Dunkeld, Bishop Toner (no relation to the author) who described the new building as 'a magnificent school'.

Most notable in the list of dignitaries were Sir Francis Norie-Miller of Cleeve, the founder of General Accident, and Mr. A. H. Gardner, the schools' inspector who had been associated with St. John's for many years and had often drawn attention to the problems of the old building. Head Teacher, Mr. James Begg, along with his wife and daughter, was present also.

A choir of St. John's pupils began the proceedings. The Chairman of Perth School Management Committee, Dr. Robert Stirling, welcomed Monsignor Turner and the guests, then with a special key presented on behalf of the contractors, Monsignor Turner formally opened the front door in Stormont Street to great applause.

In his speech Monsignor Turner stated that,

> ...the purpose of a school is to educate and, under our auspices as Catholics, we wish to bring out the best in the child, to educate the child both physically and morally and as a citizen. To produce good Christians and good citizens is the real purpose of all our schools.

After the votes of thanks, all sang the National Anthem. Guests then adjourned to the school for tea and a closer look at the superb new accommodation.

Modern facilities

Reports of the time describe the new school as having the 'most modern facilities.' The most impressive must have been the well-equipped and spacious gymnasium with its boys' and girls' changing rooms and adjacent showers while three classrooms were fitted with specialist equipment for science, domestic science and technical subjects.

The site of the new building was somewhat unusual because of the sudden and dangerous drop, halfway between front and back. Before its demolition, the front part, on Stormont Street, was occupied by St. Joseph's Convent. Twenty feet below, at

Mr Watt Allison, architect (standing) hands the keys of the school to Monsignor Turner. Facing the camera is parish priest, Canon McDaniel, who fought for the new school for many years. To his right is Sir Francis Norie-Miller, founder of General Accident (now part of Aviva) and, for a short time, Member of Parliament for Perth.

The Union Flag covering the table and the singing of the National Anthem at the close of proceedings, can only come from an earlier age.

Barossa Street, there was a private garden which was concreted over to accommodate the new school. To fit the site, therefore, the building was two storeys high at the Stormont Street end and three storeys high at Barossa Street.

The extra storey, really a basement, at the rear appears to have been planned as a male preserve. There was a boys' entrance, a boys' playground, a spacious boys' cloakroom, a technical area (a subject not open to girls until the 1980s) and a partially covered outdoor boys' toilet. The headmaster's office was next door to the cloakroom and had a good view of the playground and the janitor's room was nearby. At some point, probably very early on, the headmaster's office became the male staffroom with the headmaster moving to the top storey, where he and his successors remained ever since.

The basement is the area which changed most in the future decades and by the late 1960s all of the 1938 indoor arrangements had been altered, mostly to allow for the cooking and serving of school meals. All that remained were the boys' playground and toilets. Because of the stepped site and the construction of the boys' toilets at one end of the building only, St. John's was never able to have mixed-sex playgrounds like every other school in Britain. But there was never a complaint from any boys or from their parents.

The new school building was a local attraction as the one example of twentieth century modernity amongst the Victorian workers' houses in Stormont Street and Barossa Street and the townhouses and Georgian villas of Barossa Place. When it was complete, the more adventurous local boys shinned up the drain pipes to play football on the flat roof – much more of a challenge than street or playground.

A 1930s building

Today the St. John's building in Stormont Street seems old and out-of-date. Like many other 1930s public buildings in Scotland, it has suffered from bad decisions by councils who have shown little interest in maintaining the building in a manner sympathetic to its origins. Nevertheless, there are many surviving features which mark it out as a building of its time.

The architecture of the 1930s was based on clean horizontal and veretical lines and, in some respects, imitated the overall shape of the great liners of the period such as the *Queen Mary*. The building is seen at its best by a pedestrian approaching from the junction of Stormont Street and Atholl Street. The long side of the building shows off the clean horizontal lines made by the two main floors, one above the other, while the window frames of the classrooms emphasise the same lines. In 1990, the original frames were replaced with modern substitutes which adhered, as far as possible, to the lines created by the 1930s architect.

The strong vertical lines are at the front and rear where main doors lead upwards to tall staircase windows. They cast a gener-

ous amount of daylight onto the steep interior curved staircases which are topped with studded banisters of dark, polished wood.

Until 1993, the original flat roof was in place but flat roofs have never succeeded in the wetter Scottish climate so the well-patched St. John's version was eventually replaced with the present pitched roof.

The flat roof boasted a flagpole, another standard feature of pre-war buildings, to emphasise the structure's vertical lines. However, it was removed when the roof renovation was carried out and it's not known if it ever flew a flag.

An 'open-air' school

We've already seen that the British government became aware of the poor health of many of its young people during army recruitment for the Boer War. With the country's economy dependent on fit workers, politicians took a number of measures to improve public health. One writer described the particular problems of

A group of St. John's boys warm their hands at the workmen's brazier at the new school in June 1938.
The names of some of the boys are known: Phillip Welsh, Martin Gardiner (Smiler), Ken Lang, Gerry Alexander, Rab Doris, Jimmy Netherington, Willie Paterson (Waggie), Denis Netherington, Stewart Netherington, Unknown, Jimmy Doris, Unknown, Willie Tomlinson (Tolly), Fred Herman (Teddy), Richard Martin and David Moran.

schools: '…large numbers of school children came from insanitary slum dwellings in bare feet and carrying disease.' So, mindful of a school building as a breeding ground for disease, planners came up with the concept of the open-air school.

They expected architects to incorporate into new schools features which would protect against infection and dissipate smell as well as providing more cheerful surroundings. Sunshine, light and air would be the watchwords. Many imaginative designs were tried. The design for St. John's was one of the cheapest but it fulfilled its brief exactly. Most of the classrooms are south-facing and natural light from the tall staircase windows streamed into the stairs and corridors. Careful positioning of entrances meant that cleansing fresh air could sweep through the building when required and a row of internal windows, high on each corridor-side classroom wall, could be controlled to allow fresh-air gusts from the corridor into the room. The means for admitting light and air were admirable in their simplicity.

A new start?

All at St. John's could be forgiven for assuming that their new building, modern facilities and improvements in sanitation would herald the start of a new era. The first term in the new school began on 1st September 1938 and excellent attendances were recorded through the month but in the first week of October a wave of scarlet fever swept into the school, remaining until Christmas. Nor had problems of overcrowding been left behind in High Street. With the school leaving age due to rise to fifteen in September 1939, the education authority realised that the brand new school did not have space for an extra year group. The Second World War delayed the raising of the leaving age but when it did happen it left a problem which would dominate St. John's until well into the 1960s.

Chapter Six

Wartime (1939-1945)

Best laid schemes

The Second World War was not a surprise. Although Britain declared war on Germany on Sunday, 3rd September 1939, preparations had been underway for weeks as gas masks were issued, public buildings protected by sandbags and shops sold out of blackout material.

Two days before the war declaration, the biggest movement of people in British history got underway with the evacuation of about a million children from industrial cities across the land. The operation began at 6.30am on Friday, 1st September and by the time of Prime Minister Chamberlain's radio broadcast at 11.15am on the Sunday, it was virtually complete with the children rehoused in 'safe' areas in the countryside.

Four thousand, six hundred children from Glasgow arrived at Perth station on the evening of Saturday, 2nd September whereupon, according to *The Perthshire Advertiser*, they were:

> …marched to the various schools in the city, where they were served with emergency rations before being taken to their billets.

Accommodation had been identified six months before when volunteers undertook a survey of households and calculated how many children could be accommodated on the basis of each child under fourteeen qualifying for half a room. Perth headmasters were appointed as billeting officers to allocate children to appropriate homes and liaise with householders and the teachers accompanying the children.

Yet, despite their preparations, Perth schools were thrown into disarray by the evacuees' arrival. St. John's opened on Thursday 30th August after the summer holidays then closed again on Friday 1st September as the evacuation began. It would be four weeks before it reopened.

The problem was timing. Evacuees should have had a medical examination before leaving their home city but the eight weeks of school closure for summer meant that medicals could not be carried out in Glasgow. So the responsibility for medicals was transferred to Perth, where the few medical staff were overwhelmed and since it was difficult to communicate with the evacuees once they dispersed to their new homes, the process was very slow.

Some Perth householders were horrified when they discovered the state of their evacuees. A later enquiry acknowledged that a 'great many of the refugees…were clean, pleasant and entirely respectable people,' but it also reported that some children arrived in a 'dirty and verminous condition.' Others suffered from 'ringworm, impetigo, tubercular sores and other highly infectious complaints.' The children had been thrown into foreign surroundings and, unsuprisingly, many were confused and homesick. For some, the differences between the bustling city and the relative quiet of Perth were so acute that they could not sleep in a place of silence and darkness.

Back to normal?

Eventually the dust settled and when schools reopened on 25th September 1939, a clearer picture emerged. There were only 1500 evacuees, many of the original 4000 having returned home as parents reckoned the lack of bombs on Glasgow – until then – made it as safe as Perth.

Of the evacuees remaining, St. John's was allocated the children from St. Patrick's Boys and Girls schools in Anderston. They would be taught in their own classes. However, with the new St. John's building already overcrowded with its own 500 pupils, a plan of part-time education had to be introduced. St. John's primary pupils would attend each day from 9.00am until

12.30pm and secondary pupils from 9.00-12.30 and 2.00-4.00pm. All St. Patrick's pupils would attend from 12.30-4.00pm.

St. John's, and Southern District School in Nelson Street, were the only Perth schools that had to re-sort to part-time educa-tion. The others who received evacuees were able to accommodate their visitors more easi-

A group of St. John's prize-winners from 1943

ly, presumably because they had spare space.

This time, school managed to stay in session for two weeks. Then it was time for the potato lifting and a two-week closure.

By the end of 1939, the school was working normally along-side its complement of evacuees but their numbers dwindled and further reorganisation saw the evacuees absorbed into St. John's classes, infant, primary and secondary. By August 1940, only 60 evacuees remained accompanied by three Glasgow teachers who became part of the St. John's staff. Especially remembered is Miss Reilly 'who took no prisoners when your answers didn't come quickly enough.' (For as long as there were evacuees, there was an allocation of teachers from Glas-gow. If one was recalled, a replacement was sent.) Evacuee numbers declined throughout the war but some still remained in 1945, along with one Glasgow teacher. Eventually, the chil-dren went home but without their teacher. She decided to stay on in Perth.

First Communicants, perhaps from 1941.

Conditions excellent

Just before the war, school inspectors appeared at St. John's. It was their first visit since the new school opened so their comments had a new tone. Gone was any mention of 'depressing and miserable conditions.' 'General working conditions are excellent,' was the replacement sentence. However, there was a warning that the expected raising of the school leaving age, due in September 1939, would bring congestion and a 'need for a small relief school.'

Teaching was satisfactory but, the inspectors reported, 30% of the pupils were 'necessitous cases' and this made the work of the staff 'arduous'. In addition, difficulties were caused by an epidemic of scarlet fever. In the event, the raising of the school leaving age to fifteen was postponed until after the war. Not that it made any difference to St. John's. With the evacuees, it was overcrowded anyway.

Goodbye to our railings

Early in the war, the government announced that the public could help the war effort by donating the iron railings that bounded houses and parks.

The railings at the front of St. John's were casualties of the time and, years later, were replaced by cheap chicken wire. Railings from houses in Barossa Place were removed also but the railings at the back of the school survived. They met their end, eventually, during the 1990s. They may have survived Adolph Hitler but their short stature

Dismantling the railings around Prince Albert's statue on the North Inch in 1941. How many modern health and safety breaches can you find?

proved no match for playground football. They were replaced by higher, uglier and more effective barriers.

The wartime removal of railings deprived St John's and many other buildings of handsome decoration. It wouldn't have been so bad if the railings had been useful but the iron content was poor and many railings never got beyond the common dump.

At the time of writing, there is a move afoot to replace some of the railings removed during the war. The first stage, at the A K Bell Library, is impressive but St. John's will be long gone from Stormont Street before anyone thinks of reinstating its railings.

Change of heads

In June 1941, the headmaster, Mr. James Begg, died. He was the first male head, the first lay head and he had overseen the school's move from the dispiriting building in the High Street to the modern site in Stormont Street. He had taken on the additional post of billeting officer for evacuees at a time when he was suffering from heart trouble. It is tempting to think that his additional responsibilities hastened the end of his life.

Two months later, Mr. James Burke was appointed headmaster. A former pupil remembers him as 'something of a martinet...but maybe he needed to be.' Inspectors seemed to agree when they wrote about Mr. Burke:

...under his guidance the tone and the working spirit of the school have greatly improved.

Adjusting to war

It wasn't just schools that had trouble adjusting to a different way of life after September 1939. Many of Perth's citizens had problems too.

The carrying of gas masks was so unpopular that Lord Provost Nimmo made a speech in which he admonished citizens who refused to carry them because, apparently, they were self-conscious. He suggested that if everyone did it, no one would feel out of place.

Little is known about this photograph other than it shows a group of St. John's boys about to play football on the North Inch. It was taken in 1941 and looks as if it's an informal game at lunchtime or after school. The enthusiasm is infectious, almost seventy years later.

There were difficulties, too, in implementing the Lighting Regulations, particularly with regard to blackout arrangements. Those who had left it too late found that shops had sold out of the blackout material. The sheriff court decided to get tough and the first person prosecuted was a householder from Fairmount Drive in Perth who left an outside light burning through the night. Shamefully, he blamed it on one of his evacuees but the sheriff imposed a fine of £1 anyway. A week later, in the spirit of 'an example has to be made,' sixteen culprits appeared in court facing the £1 fine. A disproportionate number of the accused came from Crieff which appears to have been a veritable hotbed of blackout neglect. Either that, or the town had a particularly diligent police officer.

As the war progressed, other changes came into force to cope with new situations. To cope with the blackout and the injuries that were sustained due to the lack of light, the government changed the clocks. British Summer Time was used as standard time and in the summer, Double Summer Time was introduced with clocks two hours ahead of normal. The result was that evenings were long and light and mornings were dark. St. John's had to respond by changing the school hours so that the school was not breaching the blackout by using classroom lights in the morning. From then, the day ran from 9.20 – 12.10 and 1.30-4.00.

The effects of war were inside school too. Lawson Smith remembers:

> Windows had a fine mesh stuck to them to prevent flying glass in the event of bombs dropping nearby. Carrying your gas mask was a must and there were occasional practices to ensure you knew how to put it on properly. For some children this was a bit of fun but for others it could be quite claustrophobic.

Although there was much to excite children in wartime, it was a time of great anxiety too. Many St. John's pupils had fathers and brothers in the forces. Their absence would have changed family life substantially and if they were killed, as some were, children had to continue at school as normal despite their confusion and puzzlement.

By 1943, when war conditions were biting hard, the timing of the school year was changed. With men away in the Forces and women taking over their civilian jobs, the lifting of the potato crop was short of workers. So children were called upon in large numbers and schools closed for the month of October. To compensate, a month was taken from the summer holidays so that they ran for the month of July only. Children were also drafted in from other parts of the country, so important was the potato crop, and camped in vacant local schools. St. John's played host to pupils from the Sacred Heart School in Glasgow and the new potato-lifting arrangements continued for the remainder of the war.

Breaking out

Overcrowding was so acute by 1943 that extra space had to be found. The education authority owned the accommodation at the Corner House on the junction of Atholl Street and Rose Terrace and it was there that three classes of primary six and seven pupils took up temporary residence.

It may have been an outpost of the main school but it had advantages. For eleven year-old Lawson Smith the situation could not have been better.

> We watched with great interest the wooden poles being erected on the North Inch to prevent enemy gliders landing and the sound of soldiers practising their bayonet drill at the barracks drifted into the classroom. A huge Indian gong hung inside the barracks' gates and it was sounded loudly at twelve noon for the benefit of the soldiers. It also told us pupils it was near dinner time.

War ends

Increased restrictions made life more difficult as the war progressed but Perth did not suffer attacks by enemy bombers. One bomb was dropped near the Moncrieff Tunnel on June 26th 1940. The intention may have been to disrupt railway traffic or it may just have been an accident. Later, six bombs were dropped in the area of the old Perth to Stanley road. Almost certainly they were jettisoned from a German bomber returning to base after a raid elsewhere. No one was killed in either incident.

When the European war ended with the two-day *Victory in Europe* holiday on 8th and 9th May 1945, St. John's School could congratulate itself on a good war. It was one of a few schools asked to do the most in organising and accommodating evacuees and by many other means it contributed to the community and the war effort. Like the rest of Britain, it hoped for a brighter time in the post-war years. Like the rest of Britain, it was wrong.

Class photo from just after the war, probably from 1948. The setting in the boys playground looked the same sixty years later.

Two photos from just after the war, probably 1947. The wall in the Stormont Street playground never changes.

Chapter Seven

Overcrowding (1945-1967)

After the war was over

When the school year started on 1st August 1945 Britain was still at war with Japan. It took two atomic bombs to end it and with *Victory in Japan* assured, Britain celebrated with a two day national holiday on 15th and 16th August. Not to be outdone, Perth held its own victory holiday on 17th September.

British people assumed that having won the war, there would be better times ahead but their optimism didn't last long in the face of continued rationing, fuel difficulties and a bitterly cold winter in early 1947. War left the country almost bankrupt and dirty and drab from neglect.

Battling the bulge

The story of St. John's after the war is about numbers – years of serious overcrowding followed by a sudden, and dangerous, slump.

Some of it was the fault of the planners. Stormont Street was the wrong site for the 1938 building. It was full from the day it opened and the site was so restricted that there was no space for even one extra classroom.

However, the planners could not have foreseen the social effects of the ending of World War II which, in a short period, released thousands of young men from the armed forces and returned them to domestic life. Nine months later there began the biggest population explosion Britain had ever seen. The bulge, or *baby boom*, of the late 1940s and 50s ensured large

Cover of a St. John's magazine issued to celebrate the Festival of Britain in 1951.

school rolls everywhere and with ever increasing numbers, St. John's struggled to cope.

During the war the school roll of 540 had grown too large for Stormont Street so three primary classes found homes at the old Perth Academy Corner House buildings in nearby Rose Terrace. School inspectors were not impressed. They wrote:

> …these rooms are thoroughly unsatisfactory…some means will have to be found of increasing the accommodation but it must be recognised that the extreme congestion of the site will make an extension of the building a matter of great difficulty…

There was no quick response from the education authority. Two years later, in 1947, the pressure on space increased with the raising of the school leaving age to fifteen so the number of classes in the Corner House rose to six.

It took the education authority until 1952 to officially extend the school. The nearby building which had been Balhousie Boys' School (today it's St. Ninian's Primary) was renovated and

Class photograph from 1948.

Girls leaving the Stormont Street gate at the start of the 'Tattie Holidays' in October 1949. In the background is the rear of the old Perth Academy building which was used by St. John's at different times. It was demolished during the 1980s.

turned into a permanent annexe of St. John's. It had eight class-rooms and, with the transfer of classes from the 'unsatisfactory' Corner House, was full from the day it opened.

The *Perthshire Advertiser* enthused about the transformation at Balhousie, from the bright pastel shades of the redecorated corridors to 'the rose tinted fluorescent tubes which softly illuminate the wall blackboards.'

But again, the education authority was caught out. Did they not see there was worse to come? By 1952 the first children of the post-war bulge were reaching school age. And it was not a secret.

Soon the Balhousie annexe was full and it was back to the 'unsatisfactory' Corner House for one class, then another until, by 1960, four classes were again in residence. In effect, there was what we would now call a St. John's campus spanning the area

Above, winners of Norie Miller Cup and League Shield, April 1962. Back (l to r) I. Brown, P. Mackle, P. McShane, J. Melley, V. Stachlich, S. Lewrie, L. Sweeney. Front T. McIntyre, R. Doris, T. Campbell, J. Harty, C. Rioux

Football team from early 1960s

Football teams from early 1960s

Above, the Corner House which accommodated some St. John's classes between 1943 and 1967.

Below, the old Balhousie Boys' School which was the official St. John's Annexe 1945-1969. Today it is St. Ninian's Primary School.

from the Dunkeld Road to the North Inch comprising three school buildings encircling the various private residences of Barossa Place and Rose Terrace. The efficient running of the campus must have posed a special challenge to the headmasters of the time.

Then, just to keep everyone on their toes, the next development came along. With the first of the post-war bulge in their early teens, the government invented O-Grades for 4th Year pupils who did not wish to stay at school until 6th Year. So St. John's added yet another year group and this time the quest for extra space was satisfied by converting a Balhousie outhouse into a classroom.

This was to be the peak of demand for space at St. John's. There were eighteen classes between primary one and primary seven. Five were in the ground floor of the Stormont Street building, nine were at Balhousie and four were in the Corner House. The average number in each class was more than forty.

Secondary pupils occupied the top floor at Stormont Street and, for a time, an art room was situated in the old Perth Academy premises which backed onto Barossa Street.

With nowhere else to go, the education authority, in the early 1960s, made plans to relieve the St. John's roll by building two new schools. One would be a secondary school on the northern edge of the town, at Muirton, and the other would be a primary school in the large post-war housing development at Letham. St. John's itself, would take primary ages only and all would fit into the Stormont Street building.

The 'qualy' and all its devices

Things would have been worse if all the pupils finishing primary seven had stayed at St. John's but some left for other schools after the Qualifying Examination.

The 'qualy' was a standard feature of primary seven life throughout Scotland. It really wasn't one exam but consisted of several tests which claimed to measure pupils' intelligence and ability so that they could be placed in different secondary courses. These courses delighted in names like *academic* (Latin and French and no practical subjects) and *practical* (languages replaced by woodwork and metalwork for boys; domestic science and commercial subjects for girls.) No one considered that boys and girls might enjoy crossing over.

At St. John's those whom the 'qualy' deemed to be 'academic' left for Lawside Academy, Dundee, while some girls attended Kilgraston School at Bridge of Earn where the education authority paid their fees. Some children enrolled in Perth Academy instead.

A St. John's choir at the Perthshire Music Festival in the City Hall in 1953. At the very least, they deserved a prize for their smart appearance.

Forgotten photos from the back of a cupboard

The author found a small Kodak box at the back of a cupboard in Stormont Street where it had been ignored for half a century. It contained some rough *contact* prints and a few glass negatives.

The photographer is unknown but the box dates from the early 1950s and the photos may have been taken for possible inclusion in the 1951 school magazine celebrating the Festival of Britain.

Some of the photos appear on the next three pages while others are on page eighty-four.

From old glass negatives showing scenes from early 1950s. Above, gymnastic dancing; opposite page, top, an infants class and, below, science featuring Mr. J. McLaren.

Three photographs from early 1950s. Top may have been taken on the North Inch; middle appears to be a group at art. The bottom is more obvious but no other details are known of the photos.

The coming of comprehensive education in the late 1960s made the 'qualy' redundant and it disappeared from primary schools to no one's regret.

Corporal punishment

It is said that a typical Scottish education once consisted of the 'three Bs' – 'Bible, belt and blackboard'. (In a Catholic school 'Catechism' would have to replace 'Bible' with a regrettable loss of alliteration but the message is the same.)

Corporal punishment was a central feature of Scottish education although by the 1950s its use was increasingly questioned and it was eventually abolished in 1983.

Readers whose main school experience happened after 1983 will be surprised to know that the use of the belt was an everyday occurrence in Scottish schools. Most children and parents just accepted it as a normal part of school life in a time when teachers were more authoritarian and society was more deferential to all forms of authority.

However, there was one occasion when corporal punishment landed St. John's in court.

Headmaster in court

On 25th May 1949, headmaster Mr. James Burke, and a member of staff appeared in court to answer a charge made against the teacher. The story is told in the words of Mr. Burke while the teacher's name has been changed to avoid any possible embarrassment.

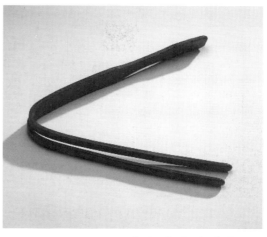

A standard school strap as known - and felt - by generations of Scottish school children until the early 1980s..

The Headmaster and Mr. D. Macdonald, teacher of English subjects in the secondary division, attended the Perth Police Court today at 9.30 am. The Headmaster was cited to appear as a witness. Mr Macdonald had to appear to defend himself on a charge of assaulting a pupil of this school. The charge was brought by the Burgh Prosecutor at the instance of the pupil's father. The action arose because Mr. Macdonald in punishing the boy, who defied him and resisted his approaches, refusing punishment on the hand in the normal way, marked the boy's buttocks with two belt marks of a light and harmless kind. The magistrate found there was no evidence of assault or excessive punishment and declared Mr. Macdonald not guilty of the charge.

Neil Macaulay got the belt

An account of corporal punishment from a former St. John's pupil, Neil Macaulay, appears on a BBC website. In this edited version the teachers' names have been changed.

When I was 11 and passed the quallie I went to St. John's R.C. in Perth for 3 years where Miss A and Miss B set up the all time world record for beltin' bairns. We got about 4 of the belt every day mostly for not knowing something. The lassies got it too but no' nearly as much as the boys. The lassies used tae start greetin' so then it would stop.

Mr Burke was the headmaster and he walked around the school wi' his belt up his sleeve. If he caught any bairn misbehaving he would flick out his arm and the belt would come whizzing

How we all looked, once upon a time. Well, those of us who were at school in the 1950s.

down into his hand and the bairn would get at least 2 of the belt on the spot.

In 1952 we all complained to our parents about the amount of homework and the belt. All our parents went to see the head and the teachers but they were as nice as pie so the parents were fooled and nothing changed.

Once Miss B lined up the whole A class (all 7 of us) and asked us what x squared was. We all knew perfectly well. We'd been doing algebra for 2 years but as each kid gave a perfectly good definition, Miss B said "Wrong" and gave 2 of the belt.

Neil Macaulay concludes that 'discipline was perfect' and 'we got the best education you could get.' He's not a fan of modern school discipline and concludes with an Old Testament quotation.

Spare the rod and spoil the child. Children will misbehave if not controlled and they won't work if they don't have to. If you think bairns are wee angels you're living in cloud cuckoo land.

Now there's a topic for debate.

The best schooldays

Many former pupils regard their St. John's schooldays fondly. The post war generation is particularly positive. 'I think our time at school was the best,' said Sally Pirie (nee Devaney) and many agree with her. In support of her case she states:

The laughs we had at school. We did work hard though and respected the teachers. Even the awful ones but there weren't many of them though.

Teachers stay in her memory clearly.

Gym scene from early 1950s showing the Stormont Street gym until 'improved' in late 1960s.

Is Mr. Thomson the art teacher still alive? He was amazing and used to let us paint our beehives purple and red streaks. My self-portrait was in the corridor for years after I left. Then there was Pop Mc-Neil, Smiler – Mr. McLaren, Ma and Pa Brennan, Clara – Mrs. McLaren, Miss McAllistair, Miss Grant, Sister Francis and Sister Louise and of course, Molly and Philly Gowrie. And Mrs. Rice, she was my primary five teacher.

I always remember the scramble to get to the cloakroom when it was a day for Benediction. Of course, we'd all forgotten our berets for our heads and it was a race to pinch anybody's off the peg or face Mrs. McLaren's wrath. Her husband, Smiler, (although he *never* smiled) was really nice though. Maybe there's a photo of him smiling somewhere?

In a newspaper cutting from 1952, the baker's roundsman sells cakes to St. John's pupils in the Balhousie playground.

And now it can be proved. Mr. McLaren *did* smile. See the St. Columba's original staff photo on page eighty four. He's fourth from the right in the front row.

Pupils from abroad

Children of immigrants have always found a place at St. John's. After the war, Irish families found work in the great hydro-electric schemes around Pitlochry while Polish families came to escape Soviet domination. There would be a second wave of Polish immigration in 2006-07 looking for work just as Italian immigrants did in the 1920s. However, Ireland started earlier than anyone with two waves in the nineteenth century: firstly, to work on the expanding railways and then as a result of the potato famine in the years following 1845.

A highlight of each year was the visit by the whole school to Kilgraston Convent at Bridge of Earn for a picnic and sports. It always took place at the end of June with everyone travelling by train. Later, transport was by means of a McLennan's bus.

Rose Mackle remembers, '...white-covered trestle tables with banks of sandwiches, ice cream and lots of excitement.'

The visits seem to have ended in the mid 1950s.

Two choir photos, both taken outside Perth City Hall. Top is from late 1950s or early 60s. Bottom is from 1966 and features Miss O'Neil, well known to generations of St. John's pupils.

Hockey team from 1948.

Under 15 football team from 1965, winners of Reilly Cup.
Back (l to r) J. Todd, C. Rioux, J. Williams, V. Zdralek, L. Sweeney, T. Campbell.
Front T. McIntyre, P. Joyce, J. Melley, S. Lewry, H. Docherty.

Top, Mr. James Burke, head-master of St. John's 1941-52. Bottom, Mr. Edmund Glover, 1952-58. After their periods at St. John's, both men emigrated.

Technology advances

The 1960s brought a rush of technology. In the 1890s the pencil sharpener came to St. John's and technology stood still for another fifty years. The new school, in 1938, came with a BBC *wireless receiver* installed and all classrooms wired for reception, thus allowing generations of St. John's pupils the peculiar delights of *Singing Together*, *Music and Movement* and *Exploring Scotland.*

The pace quickened in 1961. With the world agog as Yuri Gagarin, the first man in space, orbited the earth, St. John's acquired a *Banda* spirit duplicator. The *Banda* machine was used by teachers to produce handwritten worksheets. Writing was in purple, pink or blue and, when the machine had been over-primed and duplicator fluid soaked into its pages, classes of pupils instinctively put the fresh worksheets to their noses and inhaled deeply. In the 1980s the *Banda* was made redundant by the photocopier. For pupils it was much less interesting since its productions did not stretch to a joyful inhalation.

And so to the first St. John's television in 1963. Black and white and fuzzy but the modern world had arrived.

Leading the way

During the upheavals of the war and post-war years, St. John's was led by three formidable headmasters. Mr. James Burke (1941-1952) had been a science teacher in Cowdenbeath. He resigned in 1952 to take up a post at a school in Melbourne, Australia.

Mr. Edmund Glover (1952-1958) taught maths at Lawside Academy, Dundee, after war service and teaching around Scotland. After six years at St. John's he, too, followed the emigration route, for a post in Canada.

Mr. James Ward (1958-1967) came from war service and an early career teaching English in the Glasgow area. From St. John's he moved to St. Columba's High School on its opening and, after retiral in 1977, he remained in Perth for the rest of his life. He died in 2006 at the age of ninety-three.

Above, the St. John's fashion show of 1958 and all items made by the girls themselves. Left, an art class from 1956.

Football team from 1953 (above) and Primary Seven from 1948 (below).

Hockey teams from 1954 (above). Back (l to r) J. Mackle, V. Pattinson, M. Glover, P. Gallagher, P. O'Donnell, M. Burnett. Front, not known, I. McLaughlan, B. Connelly, E. Reoch, Y. Cardno.

Left, hockey team of unknown date.

Photos from early and mid-1950s

Chapter Eight

From One School, Make Three
(1967-1980)

St. Columba's High School opens

On the 11th April 1967, Mr. Andrew McCormack, previously head teacher at St. Stephen's, Blairgowrie, took over as head teacher at St. John's. But it was different from the St. John's which had closed for the Easter holidays only two weeks before. The two hundred secondary pupils had disappeared and on the same day were opening St. Columba's High School where they were joined by twenty staff from St. John's, including new rector, Mr. James Ward.

St. Columba's was built on the grounds of Muirton Farm at what was then the northern edge of Perth. Work had taken longer than expected so the target of opening during 1966 had been missed, an event forever commemorated on the school's badge. Designed in advance, it bore an optimistic 1966 as the date of foundation rather than the eventual 1967.

The St. Columba's badge with the inaccurate date of 1966 in the top right corner.

It was never a successful building. Signs of cost-cutting were everywhere. The lack of through corridors above ground level meant generations of pupils parading, inefficiently, down one staircase and up another just to change classes while poor space for physical education resulted in many lessons taking place off-site with consequent loss of time as well as heavy transport costs. Even the nearby ground allocated for playing fields was embargoed for fifteen years because of local objections.

Originally intended as a small school for first to third year pupils (12 to 15 year-olds), planners appeared to ignore expected developments. By the mid-1960s, the move to comprehensive secondary education was well underway throughout Scotland.

Staff photograph marking the opening of St. Columba's High School. Mr. James Ward, rector, and former headmaster of St. John's, is in front row, fourth from the left.

The likelihood of a rise in the school leaving age was widely known also so it's a mystery why the education authority (Perth and Kinross Joint County Council) approved such a poor building. Continuing its policy of transferring top-scoring second year pupils to a school in another council's area, (Dundee's Lawside Academy) was another own goal. Any ambitious authority would have wished to retain all its pupils so that a school could achieve six-year status quickly. Or did the education authority just not care?

Eventually, progress was made. The school leaving age was raised to sixteen in 1972, allowing St. Columba's to offer 'O Grade' examinations. Later, a new education authority (Tayside Regional Council) bowed to parental pressure, resulting in a full six-year school from August 1977.

The education authority's petty attitude in the 1960s imposed a serious handicap on St. Columba's. The leakage of pupils after S2 undermined its academic credentials and encouraged some parents to decide against it at primary seven, arguing that two changes of school in two years did not benefit a child.

A sewing class from 1968 or 1969. At this time domestic subjects were for girls only.

Wisely St. Columba's played to its strengths. It was small with a healthy ratio of teachers to pupils and it earned a reputation, quickly, for good pastoral care.

Our Lady's Primary School opens

After the war, Perth expanded tremendously, particularly in Letham, Tulloch and Oakbank, so it was fitting that Our Lady's primary school should be built in Letham, on a corner site beside Our Lady of Lourdes Church. It opened on 27th August 1968 with Mr. Denis Cairns, previously head teacher of St. Dominic's School in Crieff, as head teacher. Seventy pupils transferred from St. John's as did three teachers.

The Our Lady's badge from 1968 remains, more than forty years later.

Our Lady's settled quickly into its community and became a recognised force for good. The building settled also, developing a spectacular crack from one end of the top floor to the other. For years, it provided amusement to pupils with wandering concentration who could insert pencils, erasers and other small objects through the crack into the surprised classes below.

Three well-known faces from this period: Mr. A. McCormack, headteacher; Miss M. Gowrie and Miss M. Stuart. The occasion was Miss Gowrie's retiral in 1974 after 36 years at St. John's. Later, Miss Stuart was head teacher at Our Lady's for 27 years.

St. John's makes changes

Having given birth to two new schools in fifteen months, St. John's expected to benefit also. The opening of St. Columba's meant that the Corner House and old Academy were abandoned but, even after Our Lady's opened, the Balhousie Annexe was still required so that alterations could be made to St. John's. In March 1969 builders moved into Stormont Street. Areas specific to secondary education were replaced with the facilities of a modern primary school. The technical classrooms and men's staffroom in the basement were transformed into an up-to-date kitchen and two dining areas. From then on the school could provide all its pupils with hot midday meals cooked on the premises.

The redundant science and domestic science rooms became normal classrooms. However, the changes to the physical education area were more controversial. The wall bars and beams were stripped out and the boys' and girls' showers leading from each changing room were turned into stores, one for gym equipment and the other for chairs. Someone had the idea that assemblies, music and drama, as well as physical education, could be better accommodated in a 'multi-purpose' hall. Someone else described the ripping out of the gym, as 'vandalism.'

Certainly, the 'multi-purpose' hall could just as easily have fulfilled its function with wall bars, beams and

A football session from around 1978.

showers intact and the physical education programme would have benefited from them. Twelve years later the Parent Teacher Association had to raise funds to install a climbing frame with ropes and balance equipment – an updated version of the lost wall bars and beams.

A scene in the boys' playground. Date unknown but probably late 1960s or early 1970s.

The renovations took almost two years. For the school it was a lengthy disruption. The headmaster wrote,

> Teaching difficult as we are working to the noise of drills, sawing and compressors.

On the first anniversary of the builders' arrival, he noted in a tone of exasperation,

> We have forgotten what normal conditions must be like...

When workmen moved out in January 1971, the Balhousie annexe was closed and all pupils were accommodated in Stormont Street for the first time since the start of the war in 1939.

So St. John's got its share of new facilities out of the building of St. Columba's and Our Lady's but there was a serious problem around the corner.

Where did all the pupils go?

In January 1971 with everyone in the one building, the St. John's roll was around 400 pupils. After that, each year brought a decrease and by 1981 the roll dipped below two hundred – a fifty per cent drop in ten years. Early on, the headmaster wrote that,

> ...the cause is obscure as the other RC school in the district (that is, Our Lady's) shows the same pattern of decrease in roll.

Hindsight shows us the cause was not obscure. Fewer children were enrolling because, firstly, many Catholic parents were having smaller families. Secondly, while the church might advise parents to use a Catholic school, some decided, for a variety of reasons, to go elsewhere.

An overcrowded school has obvious problems but they are healthy. A declining school's problems are dispiriting. Each year there are fewer classes, fewer children and fewer teachers all working in a building with too many empty spaces and a distinct echo.

We know now that the falling roll was a prelude to a new era. The days when a Catholic school could expect parents to enrol their children automatically were gone. In future, a Catholic school would have to prove itself as good as its neighbours, if not better. For St. John's this would be the only way forward.

Below, primary seven boys showing off the puppets made at handwork, 1968. Note the traditional desks with tip up seats and personal storage space under tip up lids. The desk at bottom left also shows the pen-groove and hole for a ceramic inkwell.

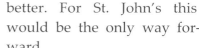

Time for new ideas

Despite its declining roll, this was also a period of innovation. Long before it was regarded as a 'good thing,' outdoor activities played a regular part in the school's life with annual camps at places like Kinloch Rannoch. They took place in holiday

St. John's School Choir at the Perthshire Music Festival, 1969.

time and were run by teachers who organised daytime expeditions then did the evening cooking with supplies they had brought from Perth. Hill walking took place on many Saturdays too.

By the mid 1960s, schools were beginning to open up to parents and St. John's was quicker off the mark than many. Parent Teacher Associations were rare but the St. John's PTA, begun in June 1967 has continued, without a break, until today. Parents' evenings to discuss children's progress began also and while St. John's parents, teachers and pupils grappled with the new attitudes required for successful parents evenings, many other schools chose to remain backward.

Along with concerts and displays, St. John's at this stage was a leader in including parents in its school life. It's a pity it was against a background of disappearing pupils.

Above and right, badminton players from 1970s.

Above, class photo, 1969, probably primary six

Left, football team from late 1960s or early 1970s.

Infant group from early 1970s.

Badminton group from late 1970s.

Chapter Nine

Struggling Through (1980-2005)

A sick building

By 1980 the "magnificent school" of 1938 was in difficulties. The building, once the most up-to-date, was in need of repair. The roof leaked, the heating system was prone to sudden breakdown and even when the heating worked the metal window frames had become so warped that they allowed extra ventilation in unexpected places. As for decoration, the combination of council tight-fistedness and a nod to 1960s psychedilia saw the corridors painted in patches of orange, purple and institutional sludge-green. The St. John's building was no longer an attractive and comfortable place for children to learn but dismal, cold and discouraging.

Let's close St. John's

The dilapidated building was a sign of deeper malaise. The school roll was falling and by 1981, it was seriously under two hundred in a school with five hundred places. The reality was that St. John's parish did not have enough children to fill the school places and if the roll's downward trend continued the school would become unviable. A few years later it would undermine St. Columba's High School too.

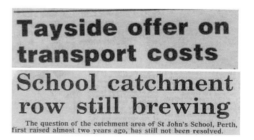

Tayside offer on transport costs

School catchment row still brewing

The question of the catchment area of St John's School, Perth, first raised almost two years ago, has still not been resolved.

Newspaper headlines from 1981 reflecting the problems of cash and catchment area.

The crisis came out of the blue and started with money. The education authority, Tayside Regional Council, claimed that the Catholic Diocese of Dunkeld owed money for years of transport to St. John's from Bridge of Earn and Scone. The Diocese denied the claim stating that it was the education authority's responsibil-

Pupils and staff of St. John's School, May 1994. (Classes Primary One to Primary Seven)

League and cup winning netball team from 1981.

ity. The school was caught in the middle.

As the dispute trundled on, the authority twisted the knife further. It was searching for extra accommodation for Perth College and hatched a plan to combine Our Lady's and St. John's into one school and gift the vacated building to the college. Council officials held school meetings with parents. At St. John's, parents wanted to keep their school but refused to vote for the closure of Our Lady's. At Our Lady's, parents also refused to vote for the closure of Our Lady's.

So the ball landed back with St. John's. It escaped closure but had to forfeit the ground floor classrooms to Perth College. The education authority's lack of sympathy reinforced the impression that they hoped St. John's would continue to shrink, thus allowing the college to take over more space. Eventually, the school would die.

Recovery begins

But the school was tougher than that and the authority's expectations did not work out. The roll began to recover and to need more space, so the accommodation sharing ended in 1989.

The recovery was not an accident. The education authority was right: St. John's did have a problem because the numbers it required no longer existed within St. John's Parish.

The school's headteacher knew that pupils would have to be attracted from beyond the Catholic community if it was to have a future and it happened through the activities of the enthusiastic but underused Parent Teacher Association.

The PTA's campaign to see off Perth College may have failed but it pulled everyone together and gave its members a greater involvement in the school. Membership increased to the extent that, at its peak, even its Annual General Meeting filled the school hall to overflowing and all its activities fostered a strong climate of support for the school.

In 1980s Perth, few schools could boast of a PTA so St. John's parents, with their closer knowledge of their school, spread their satisfaction by word of mouth.

League winning football team from 1981

The school's reputation grew and soon parents beyond the Catholic community began enrolling their children.

The challenge for the school was to ensure that its positive reputation was genuine and based on good attitudes to children and their achievements.

Building a new roll

The roll started its increase, in a small way, as early as 1983 and continued for the next twenty years until there was no room left.

For a while it brought only good. More pupils meant more money and more teachers. The school's growing confidence also meant that it was amongst the first to take on new (and worthwhile) initiatives such as a nursery class in 1990, teaching French to primary six and seven pupils and running its own finances. (It seems strange, now, that until the early 1990s, schools had no control over their own budgets. Education authorities preferred to do it themselves. It gave them more power.)

In time, more pupils brought more problems, too. Pressure on space became acute especially in playgrounds, dining halls and gymnasium. With every room needed as a classroom, there was no opportunity to have the library or computer suite that was becoming common in other schools. By 2005 with the roll around

400, even cloakrooms and lunch rooms were commandeered for small groups and instrumental music teaching. But difficulties are relative and any school prefers the problems of too many children to the problems of too few.

The 'secret' local school

With St. John's parish lacking the children to fill the school, where did the growing roll come from? In August 1986, something important happened that mostly went unnoticed. A five year-old boy started school at St. John's but, most importantly, he was not a Catholic. His friend who lived next door was a Catholic and attended St. John's so, for his parents, it was logical that their son should go there too.

Above, five-a-side football, 1982. Below, the Flying Goalkeeper, for many years a popular feature of the boys' playground. The artist is seated, centre, wearing his jumper, 1997.

From that small beginning, other families in the area who were not Catholics began sending their children. By 2005, forty-four per cent of St. John's pupils were not Catholics but were happily part of the school community, playing a full part in the school, including its religious life.

Some of the cast of Helen Come Home, June 1988

Eventually, St. John's contained more local children than the official local school did. That St. John's had, in effect, become the real local school was a delightful twist of fate which the education authority, and the Church too, found easiest to ignore.

Since the mid-1980s, another factor contributed to the the rise in St. John's numbers: the growing number of Catholic children who came from outside the official St. John's catchment area. Different families had different reasons for passing other schools but by 2005 their children made up thirty-one per cent of the St. John's roll.

What the new roll was about

The turnaround in the school roll between the mid-1980s and 2005 was necessary for St. John's to survive. It was also necessary for St. Columba's High School to survive. With St. John's the main contributor to St. Columba's it is no surprise that seven years after the St. John's roll was at its lowest ebb, education officials were

Girls' playground, mid-1980s. Stormont Street flats in the background.

Previous page, top, playground faces from the mid 1990s; below, class photo, Primary Seven, 1983.

considering the possibility of closing St. Columba's. The St. John's recovery contributed to a St. Columba's recovery and by 2005 both schools had accommodation difficulties because of the pressure of pupil numbers.

However, the St. John's growth shows that it changed from simply being a Catholic school for parish children. At 2005, only twenty-five per cent of its pupils came from St. John's parish and if the school relied on the parish alone, it would be more unviable than it was in 1983.

If St. John's – at primary and secondary stages from 2009 – is to continue to thrive, it must foster and encourage the three-way alliance of parish children, children who are not Catholics and Catholics from beyond its catchment area, that brought about its astonishing recovery. To lose any of these groups would be a serious mistake which would affect the health of not just the primary department but the secondary department too.

Mock election candidates and supporters, 1997.

A school once in the doldrums and near to closure, now overflows with enthusiastic children but the recovery was not an accident.

The brief return of Bishop Rigg

When Bishop George Rigg, the official founder of St. John's School, died in 1887, he was buried, with much ceremony, in the Lady Chapel behind St. John's Church. Almost a century later he was back.

The Lady Chapel had fallen into disuse and become the St. John's parish hall. There, on Wednesday evenings, the cub scouts played indoor football oblivious to the inscribed brass plate in the floor marking the bishop's burial place. By 1980 the hall was derelict and due for demolition to make way for a replacement but before the wreckers moved in, Bishop Rigg's coffin was dug up. It was placed in a new coffin and taken on the short journey into the church he had known so well, to lie before the High Altar. Requiem Mass was said and amongst the large congregation were staff, pupils, former staff and former pupils of St. John's School who came to pay tribute to their school's co-founder.

Later that day, Bishop Rigg's body was reburied in Perth's Welshill Cemetery where it now rests.

Growing staff numbers too

Once, schools were staffed by teachers, helped by a secretary and janitor if they were fortunate, but all that changed during the 1980s and 90s. The added demands and complications of school life meant a clutch of new posts and titles.

In February 1993, St. John's Primary Six and Seven classes presented a thirty minute television programme as a Sunday Service. It was recorded in St. John's Church and included music, drama and reflections on the Perth floods which took place earlier in the same month. After transmission, complimentary letters arrived from all over Britain.

Auxiliaries and classroom assistants took on many non-teaching tasks; learning assistants gave additional help to individual pupils and playground supervisors tried to regulate playground behaviour and prevent accidents. As in other schools, the staff of St. John's became a group of adults with different experiences and qualifications, each playing their part in the school's life.

Outdoors at Dalguise

Each year primary seven pupils set out for a week of outdoor activities and not a year was missed. The first, in 1984, was a skiing trip to Newtonmore. After that there were annual visits to

Primary Seven, 1993.

Dalguise House near Dunkeld although in the late 1980s two visits were made to Nethy Bridge in Inverness-shire when Dalguise was closed for renovation.

Dalguise House was run by children's adventure company PGL. It had the advantage of being far enough away for children to feel that they had left home behind without breaking the bank for transport costs. At Dalguise, children experienced challenging activities which are otherwise beyond the resources of schools, with sessions on abseiling, archery, raft-building, climbing, quad-biking, fencing, assault course and orienteering, along with other activities usually involving mud and water. Equally important was enjoying the ups and downs of relationships with their class-mates and teachers for twenty four hours a day, especially for the many children for whom Dalguise was the longest period they had been away from their parents.

As a bonus, primary seven pupils from Our Lady's came too so that children from both schools could meet before attending St.

Columba's High School in the following year.

There were some changes over the years. Safety was always paramount but as it became ever more stringent, some activities became less adventurous. Then there was the advent of the mobile phone which allowed a child to talk to parents at home, instantly. Helpful when only a word of reassurance was required but it could also diminish one of the aims of outdoor education – the growth of independence.

Some things never changed. Most children were too excited for sleep on the first night and appeared pale-faced the next morning. Teachers knew that the sweets were hidden under mattresses and pillows but pretended they didn't. All the boys became hoarse and some lost their voices while, on the Friday afternoon, adults and children alike returned to school exhausted.

Netball champions 2004

Typical Dalguise faces from 1998

The building recovers

In the early 1990s the building was given a face lift to help it cope with middle age. Out went the depressing 1970s décor and in came light, fresh colours. Window frames were replaced, keeping as close to the original lines as possible and, with a new boiler installed, heating costs fell. The leaky flat roof was replaced with a pitched roof which detracted from the 1930s appearance but was better adapted to the Perthshire climate.

While the St. John's building would never regain its 1938 magnificence, its upgrading meant that school was a more pleasant experience for teachers and pupils. Schools winning responsibility for their own budgets meant that repairs and decoration could be done regularly so that the building would never reach such a low ebb again.

By 2000, there were new problems as the school reached its maximum roll and expectations about modern primary school accommodation changed. A paint job would not improve matters and, as ever, the tightness of the site ruled out any extension or alteration. It looked as if teachers, children and parents would have to do their best within the building as it stood.

Updating our appearance

In 1982, the school introduced a new badge and tie. The old colours had become a liability since they were too close to those of another school and several occasions of being blamed for the other school's poor behaviour meant time for a change.

Below, Primary Seven on a backstage tour of Perth Theatre, 1992

Cast of Ali Baba, June 1998

The new badge was designed by Mrs. Lois Macdonald, the school's art teacher and was packed with symbolism. The 16th century Maltese Cross of St. John the Baptist is the central feature with a red background commemorating the shedding of his blood for his belief in Jesus. The lettering of *St. John's* is in the style of the Book of Kells, a medieval Celtic manuscript of the four Gospels.

In the lower part, the book of learning is set in the waters of the River Tay, illustrating that our learning comes from our community and is, in turn, used for the community's benefit.

The school tie was designed by another art teacher, Mr. Steve Willing, and employed the main colours of the badge. Twenty-eight years later Mr. Willing admitted that he had failed to make an exact match between the silver of the badge and the silver of the tie. And none of us noticed.

The St. John's badge from 1982 to 2009.

'All the world's a stage…'

All children should have the chance to perform on a public stage. The range of experiences they meet – voice, movement, music,

dance, teamwork, commitment, rhythm, audience awareness, memory, improvisation, stage presence – provide such a boost to their confidence that their other school learning benefits long after the laughter and applause has faded.

For many children 'putting on a show' is one of their most formative and powerful experiences, still remembered in detail in adulthood. Andrew Taylor saw it as a promotion to go from the chorus of the 'marvellous' *Ragged Child* to the thrill of his 'big part' as Muff Potter in *Tom Sawyer* .

The school facilities were not encouraging. There was no theatre, stage or drama studio and, at the best of times, the

Older children at a lunch-time running event, late 1980s.

electrics could be problematic. But the annual conversion of the gym into a makeshift theatre was achieved at no greater cost than a few jammed fingers and usually the lighting succeeded even if frequent finger-crossing and fuse-mending were required.

Plays were chosen for the scope they gave the actors and for their entertainment value but it was important, also, that they appealed to boys.

Unless they are encouraged, many boys shy away from music and drama but where a school is convinced of their value, it must make it attractive for boys to take part. The ideal is that the boys who roll around in the mud of a football pitch on one day should

Top, laughing footballers from 1994. Bottom, the author at work, late 1980s.

turn up to rehearse a song or dance just as enthusiastically on the next. It was an ideal which St. John's achieved many times over, as a glance at this chapter's photographs will show.

For boys and girls the greatest sign of their commitment was that most rehearsals took place during their own time in the lunch break or after school. Anyone joining just for the fun of getting out of class would have been disappointed.

Some plays presented particular problems. Any story about Troy requires a wooden horse to hold the Trojan army; Sweeney Todd's victims have to be tipped from his barber's chair into the basement pie shop; Jack and the Beanstalk needed a dancing highland cow. (No, I can't remember why.) Of course the fun was in overcoming the obstacles, usually with the help of talented parents.

For the erstwhile child actors – and their parents – here is the list of productions which the school mounted over twenty-five years:

The Wooden Horse (1983) Carrots (1984) Smike (1985) The Machine Gunners (1985) Oliver! (1987) Ernie's Incredible Illucinations (1987) Helen Come Home (1988) A Christmas Carol (1988) The Ragged Child (1989) Tom Sawyer (1990) The Evacuees (1991) Three One Act Plays (1992) Oliver! (1993) The Sweeney Todd Shock 'n' Roll Show

(1994) The Dracula Spectacula (1995) The Evacuees (1996) Rats! & Let's Put on a Show (1997) Ali Baba (1998) The Rocky Monster Show (1999) Jack and the Beanstalk (2000) Ernie's Incredible Illucinations (2001) Joseph and the Amazing Technicolor Dreamcoat (2002) Zoom! (2003) Androcles and the Lion (2004) You are a Star (2005) Hoodwinked (2006) Bugsy Malone (2007) Aristocats (2008) Jungle Book (2009)

Inspectors call

In 1998, school inspectors arrived in St. John's on a visit which would set the seal on the work of the previous eighteen years. For a week they examined all of the school's life under twenty-two headings and then pronounced judgement. All aspects of the school fell into their top two categories. Thirteen, such as *quality of teaching, quality of pupils' learning* and *use of assessment* were 'good'. Nine others, including *the school's ethos, the structure of the*

'Oliver!' requires a coffin which the local funeral directors were happy to provide. However, when a squad of twelve year-old boys cheerfully carried the coffin to school, they stopped the traffic in nearby Barossa Place as motorists gawped at the sight and wondered what new punishment had been invented.

Informal class photograph of Primary Seven, summer 1981. It includes an image of the (much younger) author

curriculum and *the effectiveness of leadership and promoted staff* were 'very good'. None was 'fair' or 'unsatisfactory'.

Inspectors also listed St. John's key strengths:

> Overall high quality provision for children's development and learning in nursery; a very good ethos, strong partnership with parents and links with the community; high quality assemblies and ample opportunities for religious observance; happy, very well-behaved pupils who enjoyed very good relationships with their teachers; hard working and committed staff who provided high levels of pastoral care; clear and supportive leadership from the headteacher and his management team.

In a private remark, inspectors said that they would be very happy to have their own children attend St. John's. This, they said, was their personal test of a school and many did not pass.

On the subject of compliments, even a trawl of the internet can find this comment from a former pupil of the late 1980s:

> The days I spent at St. John's were very good in terms of education, a religious and moral grounding and, above all, great fun...I'm forever grateful for having gone (there).

Who could ask for anything better?

Left, footballers from 1999; right netball from 1997

Left, from 1989; below left from 1988 and below, from 1999.

This page, some St. John's faces from 1982 to 2001. Opposite page: cast of 'Evacuees' 1996; visiting 'Discovery,' Dundee 1994; netball winners 1998; scene from 'Tom Sawyer' 1900.

Clockwise from top right: footballers 2003; Rotary quiz champions, 2000; winners of Norie-Miller cup, 2004; brass players, 1997; winners of Diocesan football tournament, 1989; cross-country running champions, 1996.

Chapter Ten

New Century, New School
(2005 onwards)

On the move again

When the news came, it was a complete surprise. In early 2003, Perth and Kinross Council announced a programme of new schools. Six campuses would be built to replace buildings which were past their best. On the list were the words:

> A new Roman Catholic Campus will be built on an extended site where St Columba's High School is currently situated. It will replace the existing St John's Primary and St Columba's High School... It should open in August 2007.

Our Lady's Primary School was included in the original proposal but the school's parents did not wish to take part.

The schools would be designed, built and operated by a partnership between Perth and Kinross Council and a private industry consortium and the replacement for St. Columba's and St. John's would take pupils across the age range from 3 to 18. Eventually, and after consultation, the new school acquired a name. It would be called St. John's Academy, which allowed it to retain its historic links to Perth.

St. John's Academy was planned for 50 nursery places, 350 at primary and 650 at secondary. Later the primary numbers were increased to 418.

The council gave many assurances, in the early days, that the new school would open in August 2007 and that there would not be any possibility of the project slipping. But 2007 came and went without any visible action. The cutting of the first turf was in February 2008 at an on-site ceremony attended by invited guests and pupils from St. Columba's and St. John's. Bishop Vincent Logan cut the turf and construction commenced immediately.

Due to the need to demolish the St. Columba's building, the school would be built in two stages. The first, due for completion in 2010, would be the secondary classroom block and associated

This 2008 photo shows building underway on the site of the new St. John's Academy. In the centre left is the curve of the secondary teaching block with the spinal 'street' which runs from one end of the campus to the other. At the centre right is the St. Columba's building which was demolished in 2010 to make way for the circular primary building and its attached nursery.

areas then, with secondary pupils moved into their new accommodation, the old St. Columba's building would be demolished and the site used for the nursery and the circular primary block. By October 2011 the whole school would be together in its new building.

However, St. John's Academy was underway before then. It became reality in August 2009. Although the previous buildings remained, new titles and a new uniform marked a new school in the making. St. John's Academy, Primary Campus, would be in Stormont Street with St. John's Academy, Secondary Campus, at Malvina Place and pupils would be sporting a new tie and badge (or 'logo' as modern, commercially-aware children call it.)

While a new uniform would help pupils identify with their new school, the moulding of one school out of two would demand herculean efforts by head teacher and staff. It would be the most demanding task of St. John's Academy's early years.

At a special Mass on 24th June 2009 (Feast of St. John the Baptist) pupils from St. John's Primary and St. Columba's High Schools joined together to mark the start of St. John's Academy.

Monsignor Charles Hendry blessed the new colours.

New Badge

The St. John's Academy badge incorporates symbols of the school's previous traditions. The celtic cross of St. John the Baptist comes from the first St. John's badge, the waters of Baptism (or is it the River Tay?) from the second one and the motto, 'Seek the Good' from St. Columba's.

The St. John's badge from 2009.

Pressure increases

During 2004, Poland became a member of the European Union, an act which directly affected the St. John's roll. With Perth a popular destination for migrating Polish families, St. John's found itself welcoming Polish pupils. A few arrived during 2004 but a year later Polish children comprised one-fifth of the school roll.

Polish children are assets to any school because of their positive attitudes to behaviour and learning but their sudden appearance put even more pressure on a building that was already full. At least, the education authority could claim to have been far-seeing and point to its plans for a replacement school. By then, it couldn't come quickly enough.

Above, a (rather poor) newspaper photo of the Stormont Street building taken one month before it opened in 1936. Right, the same building in June 2009. The main differences are the new roof and the markings and equipment in the playground.

Mr. Mackay's Legacy

James Mackay and, later, Bishop George Rigg, lived in poverty as did their parishioners. Unlike founders of private schools, they had no fortunes to leave but they took a practical approach to St. John's School and were determined that poverty should not deny children the education which would improve their lives.

While the removal of Catholic schools from church control in 1918 was a life-saver, it wiped out direct parish responsibility and

ended a line of hard-working parish priests and parishioners. Despite that, St. John's continued to thrive. Today's catchment arrangements mean that, at primary ages, St. John's draws from a social background wider than any other Perth school and the resulting mix of pupils is often seen as one of the school's strengths.

When James Mackay died in 1884, the documents relating to his Will mentioned his work at Murthly, Blairgowrie and Tullimet and in Leicestershire. But there is no mention of Perth or his work in education. It's as if it was so long before, that it didn't matter. He could not have foreseen that his small venture would be alive and well almost two centuries after he began it, still striving to provide a good education for children from all backgrounds.

An apt choice for the final photo of the chapter. Taken in December 2009, pupils of St. John's Academy perform a concert of Christmas music. The ages range from Primary Six to Secondary Six - after less than a term, it is obvious that everyone belongs to the one school.

A photograph to send us away laughing. A sports day wheelbarrow race from an unknown date, perhaps late 1960s or early 70s. Determination to win means bundling the 'barrow' over the line at all costs.

Appendix 1   Head Teachers of St. John's School, Perth (from 1860)

St. John's RC School (1860-1947; ages 5-12 then 5-13 then 5-14)
St. John's RC Junior Secondary (1947-1967; ages 5-15 then 5-16)
St. John's RC Primary School (1967-2009; ages 5-12 then 3-12)
St. John's Academy (2009; ages 3-18)

1860 – 1862	Miss Douglas
1862 – 1865	Miss Mary Cattanach
1865 – 1874	Miss Mary Jane Smith (Sister Mary Elizabeth)
1874 – 1886	Miss Mary Potts (Sister Mary Teresa)
1889 – 1889	Miss Mary Winifred Swan
1889 – 1900	Miss Annie Fay
1900 – 1903	Miss Elizabeth Thornton (Sister Mary Paul)
1903 – 1905	Miss Mary E. Hickey (Sister Mary Cordula)
1905 – 1910	Miss Mary L. Ord (Sister Mary Ambrose)
1910 – 1919	Miss Helen Coutts (Sister Mary Winifrede)
1919 – 1924	Miss Maria Morley (Sister Mary Philomena)
1924 – 1941	Mr. James Begg
1941 – 1952	Mr. James Burke
1952 – 1958	Mr. Edmund J. Glover
1958 – 1967	Mr. James J. Ward
1967 – 1980	Mr. Andrew McCormack
1980 – 2005	Mr. Brian Toner
2005 – 2009	Mrs. Bernadette Scott
2009	Mrs. Audrey May

Appendix 2   Head Teachers of St. Columba's High School, Perth

1967 – 1977	Mr. James J. Ward
1977 – 1990	Mr. Thomas Kane
1990 – 2006	Mr. Daniel McGinty
(2003-2005	Miss Carol Gillespie)
2007 – 2009	Mrs. Cecilia Flanigan (School closed July 2009)

Appendix 3   Parish Priests of St. John the Baptist, Melville Street, Perth

1830-1832	Rev. John Geddes
1832-1846	Rev. James Mackay
1846-1856	Rev. Dr. John McCorry
1856-1864	Rev. Dr. George Rigg[1]
1864-1869	Rev. Dr. John Macpherson
1869-1871	Rev. Patrick McManus
1871-1877	Rev. William Smith[2]
1877-1878	Rev. Joseph Holder
1878-1885	Rev. William Geddes[3]
1885-1902	Very Rev. John Canon Turner[4]
1902-1913	Very Rev. Michael Canon Lavell
1913-1920	Rev. Thomas Walsh
1920-1939	Rev. John McDaniel
1939-1971	Rt. Rev. Mgr. John Coogan
1971-1981	Very Rev. Derby Canon Melloy
1981-1987	Rev. Edward Durkin
1987-1992	Rev. Charles Adamson
1992-2009	Rt. Rev. Mgr. Charles Hendry
2009-	Rev. Tom Shields

1   Later, Bishop of Dunkeld 1878-1887
2   Later, Archbishop of St. Andrew's and Edinburgh 1885-1892
3   Bishop Rigg also resided at St. John's during his period as Diocesan Bishop, 1878-1887
4   Bishop James Smith, Bishop Rigg's successor as Bishop of Dunkeld (1890-1900), also resided at St. John's for a time. In 1894 he moved to Dundee where the Bishops of Dunkeld have resided ever since. Bishop Smith became Archbishop of St. Andrew's and Edinburgh in 1900.

Appendix 4 Former pupils of St. John's School
who gave their lives during the First World War (1914 – 1918)

The *Roll of Honour,* below, was published in the Minutes of Perth School Board dated 4th February, 1916. Since the worst of the war was still to come at the Somme and Passchendale, we can be certain that many other former pupils of St. John's lost their lives in this 'war to end all wars'.

Roll of Honour

Being the names of those past scholars of this School who, in Lord Kitchener's appeal for King and Country, saw the gleam of his duty and followed it.

Archibald Allan, Patrick Allan;

Thomas Brown, John Boyle;

Thomas Cairney, Henry Conlin, George Cushnie, John Costello, Francis Cassidy, John Coyne, Thomas Coyne, James Coyne, John Coleman, William Chalmers;

Patrick Dalton, Thomas Dalton, William Drummond, Thomas Doris, Edward Doris (Black Watch), Edward Doris (Royal Engineers), Bernard Doris, Joseph Dolan, William Dolan;

Peter Fachie, William Ferry, Stephen Foley, Daniel Foley, Thomas Foley, Hugh Foley, George Foy, John Flynn, James Flynn, Michael Flynn (Black Watch), Michael Flynn (17th Royal Scots), Patrick Flynn, Austin Flynn, William Forbes, Patrick Ford, Michael Feeney, Patrick Folan;

Edward Greig, Joseph Gannon, John Gannon, Donald Gannon, Thomas Gannon, John Gannon, John Gillies, Aneas Gavin, Michael Gilooly, Daniel Gardiner;

Alex Herman, Robert Hall, Thomas Hoolahan, Patrick Holland, James Hobin, William Hobin, Patrick Higgins (Highland Light Infantry), Patrick Higgins (South African field Forces), George Hagggart, Thomas Hennachin, Patrick Hennachin;

Peter Kane, John Kerrigan, Jas. Kerrigan, James Kerrigan, Hugh Kerrigan, John Kerrigan, Daniel Kerrigan, John Kelly;
John Lynagh, James Low, John Low, Michael Leyden, Edward Love, Edward Lang, Thomas Lang, Archibald Lowrey, John Lowrey;

Peter McDougall, George McDougall, Patrick McInally, Peter Murphy, James Melloy (Black Watch), James Mahoney, John McLaughlan, Patrick McGuire, Patrick McMahon, John Melloy, Patrick Melloy, Peter Melloy, Peter Melloy, James Melloy, (3rd Royal Scots), Robert McAuley, Patrick Maley, John Maguire, Alex Maguire,

Robert McKernan, Thomas McKernan, James McKendrick, James McLaughlin, James Murra, James McCabe, Patrick McCabe, George McCabe, Alex McCabe, John Maley, James McMahon, Patrick McMahon, J J Murray, James Murray, Peter Murray Thomas McLaughlan, John Mackie, Thomas Mullen, John Maley (Black Watch), Robert McGinn, Andrew McCusker, George McCrae, Mark Moran;

John Nolan;

John O'Neill, Matthew O'Neill;

Chas. Peterson, Joseph Peterson;

Patrick Quinn, John Queen;

Chas. Rennet, Michael Reilly, John Reilly, Michael Reilly, John Reid, George Reid, William Robertson, Austin Reilly, William Rennet, John Reilly, Alex. Robertson, Edward Robertson, Robert Robertson, John Robertson, Allan Rowley;

Thomas Smith, William Smith, Joseph Smith, Frank Stewart, John Sime, Thomas Sime, Daniel Sime, James Sime, Edward Scott, Robert Stewart, Alex. Stewart, Thomas Somerville, Thomas Stanton, Joseph Schindler, Peter Spellman, Matthew Spellman, Philip Spellman;

Hugh Taylor, John Taylor, Patrick Thorpe;

Thomas Welsh;

From Perth School Board minutes 1914-1919 vol 1 pp.777 – 779. (The School Board Minutes also include rank and regiment.)

Bibliography

Anderson, R.D. *Education and the Scottish People 1750-1918* (Oxford: Oxford University Press, 1995)

Anon. *The Sacred Heart - a Glimpse of the First Fifty Years* (Edinburgh, 1901)

Berry, George *Discovering Schools* (Tring: Shire Publications, 1970)

Calder, Angus *The People's War* (London: Jonathan Cape, 1969)

Devine, T.M. *The Scottish Nation 1700-2000* (London: Allen Lane The Penguin Press, 1999)

Duncan, Jeremy *Perth A Century of Change* (Derby: Breedon Books, 2008)

Fothergill, R. *What's in a Name? A survey of Perth Street Names* (Perth: Perth Civic Trust, 1979)

Gardiner, Julie *Wartime: Britain 1939-1945* (London: Headline, 2004)

Graham-Campbell, D. *Perth, the Fair City* (Edinburgh: John Donald, 1994)

Lavelle, Michael *Historical Sketch of the Perth Mission 1832-1907* (Perth, 1907)

Longmate, Norman *How We Lived Then* (London: Hutchinson, 1971)

Maclean, K. (editor) *An Environmental Atlas of Perth* (Perth 1979)

McKean, Charles *The Scottish Thirties* (Edinburgh: Scottish Academic Press, 1987)

Paterson, Lindsay *Scottish Education in the Twentieth Century* (Edinburgh: Edinburgh University Press, 2003)

Schnitker, Harry (editor) *A New History of the Catholic Community and Parish of Perth* (Edinburgh: Aquhorties Press, 2007)

Smout, T.C. *A Century of the Scottish People* (London: Collins, 1986)

Stavert, Marion L. *Perth A Short History* (Perth: Perth & Kinross District Libraries, 1991)

Steel, Tom *Scotland's Story* (London: Collins, 1984)

Stephens, W.B. *Education in Britain 1750-1914* (London: Macmillan, 1998)

University of the Third Age *The War Years in Perth* (Perth: Perth & Kinross District Libraries, 1989)

Wicks, Ben *No Time to Wave Goodbye* (London: Bloomsbury, 1988)

Articles
Kenneth, Brother, *The Education (Scotland) Act 1918 in the Making* (Innes Review vol.19, 1968)

Treble, J.H. *The Development of Roman Catholic Education in Scotland 1878-1978* (Innes Review vol.29, 1978)

Other Documents
House of Commons, *Returns of the amount of subscriptions etc* (London, 1862)

Committee of Council on Education *Report 1861-62* (HMSO, 1862)

Leslie's Directory for Perth and Perthshire (various years)

Perthshire Advertiser

Perthshire Constitutional

St. John's School, Perth *Logbooks 1864-1982*

St. John's School, Perth *Admission Registers 1925-1970*

Online
Scotsman Archive

SCRAN

National Archives, London

Maps
Perth 1860, Ordnance Survey Map (National Library of Scotland 2004)

Perth 1901, Ordnance Survey Map (Alan Godfrey Maps, Durham 1987)

Photograph Credits

Perthshire Advertiser: 2 (lower), 66 (upper), 69, 79, 80, 86 (upper) 97, 98 (upper), 102, 106, 114 (thrd. top on rt.),122

Louis Flood, Perth (including Cowper & Co.): 2 (upper), 77 (lower), 81 (upper)**,** 94-95, 96, 107

Courtesy and © D.C.Thomson & Co., Ltd Dundee: 85, 86 (lower), 87, 108-109

H. Tempest Ltd.: 62, 64, 100

A K Bell Library Local Studies / Perthshire Advertiser: 36, 46, 47, 49, 52, 55, 57, 58, 75, 78

A K Bell Library Local Studies: 44 (upper)

Author's Collection: 30, 44 (lower), 68, 70, 71, 72, 74 (lower), 98 (lower), 99, 103, 104, 105, 110 (upper), 111, 112, 114 (except third top on right), 115 (all), 116 (all), 120

National Archives, London: 11

©National Library of Scotland. Licensor www.scran.ac.uk: 13

© Perth Museum and Art Gallery. Licensor www.scran.ac.uk: 25, 65

© RCAHMS. Licensor www.rcahms.gov.uk: 27

©National Museums Scotland. Licensor www.scran.ac.uk: 73

Courtesy of Andrew Mitchell: 21, 119, 121

Courtesy of Roben Antoniewicz: 74 (upper), 111 (lower)

St. John's Academy, Perth: 84

Laing O'Rourke Construction: 118

Perth Museum and Art Gallery: 43

Thanks to www.weareperth.co.uk: 51, 101

Index

Begg, James   39, 57
Blairgowrie   5, 28
Burke, James   58, 73, 78

Catholic Church   1
Catholic schools, equalising of pay   39
Catholic schools, transferred to govt.   38
Cattanach, Mary   6, 9, 10, 11, 12, 13, 14, 18
Church of Scotland   19
Cistercian monks   29
Crieff   5, 12, 59, 85
Cumming, Rev. Mr.   15
Curriculum
        Arithmetic   25
        Expansion   28
        Reading   27
        Scottish History   11

Dalguise near Dunkeld   103
Diphtheria   16
Douglas, Miss   9, 10, 12
Drummond Stewart, Sir William   5
Dundee   21
        Lawside Academy   69
Dunkeld, Bishops of
        Logan, Rt. Rev.Vincent   117
        Macfarlane, Rt. Rev. Angus   35
        Rigg, Rt. Rev. George See Rigg, Rev.
        George
        Toner, Rt. Rev. John,   48
Dunkeld, Diocese of   20, 93

Edinburgh
        Edinburgh Chapel Choir   4
        St. Mary's Cathedral   7
        St. Mary's School   7
Education (Scotland) Act 1872   18
Education (Scotland) Act 1918   37, 39
Education in Scotland   4

Fairs   16
Feeing markets   16
Finance

Fund-raising   24
Funding   17, 22, 23
Grant reduction   36
Grants   9, 17
Parish contribution   9
Pay in Board schools   23
Pay of Catholic teachers   23, 35
Payments to schools   22
Staffing costs   23
Free Church of Scotland   19

Gardner, A. H. HMI   48
Geddes, Rev. John   3
Glover, Edmund   78
Grandtully   28

Hendry, Rt. Rev. Mgr. Charles   119
Highland Perthshire   12, 28

Influenza   16, 28
Insurance, Scottish Widows   3
Ireland   7

Kilgraston School   69
King Edward VII   31, 43
Knox, John   1

Lady Chapel, St. John's Church   101
Lafferty, Mr   5
Little Dunning Fair   16
Lynch J. HMI   12, 15

Macdonald, Dr. Mary   39, 40
Macdonald, Lois   105
Mackay, Rev. James   3, 4, 5, 28, 29, 120
Macpherson, Rev. John   13, 14
McCormack, Andrew   83, 86
McCorry, Rev. John   5, 6, 7, 8, 9, 18
McKeown, Mr   5
Measles   28
Mother Mary Angela   14
Mount St. Bernard's Abbey, Leics.   29

Murthly Chapel 5
Murthly Estates 5, 28
Murthly, Laird of 5

Napoleonic Wars 5

O'Hara, Mr 5

Parish priests, role of 24, 38
Payment by results 22, 24
Peeling the oak 17
Perth
    Balhousie Boys' School 64
    Barossa Place 57
    Barossa Street 14
    Burghmuir 17
    Carpenter Street 6, 9
    Central District School 34
    Greig's Close 5
    High Street 5, 6, 8, 9
    In 1860 8
    Irish Migrants 8
    King Edward Street 31, 43, 44
    Letham 85
    Lowe's Dancing Academy 6, 9
    McNab's Shoe Shop 9
    Meal Vennel 6, 8, 32, 42, 44
    Melville Street 3, 4, 6, 9
    Mercat Cross 43
    Muirton Farm 83
    North Inch 60
    Oakbank 17
    Our Lady's Primary School 85, 96, 103
    Perth Academy 4, 5
    Perth Prison 8, 12, 13
    Reformation 1, 3
    Seven Star Close 5
    Shuttlefield Close 25
    Slum Clearance 42
    South Street 8
    Southern District School 55
    St. Columba's High School 75, 83, 93, 103, 117
    St. John's Centre 44
    St. John's Square 44

St. Johnstone FC 1
St. John's Catholic Church 6
St. John's Centre 8
St. John's Kirk 1
St. Joseph's Convent 14, 42
Stormont House 14
Stormont Street 14, 42, 46, 50, 63
Stratton's Confectioners 32
Wartime evacuees 54
Perth and Kinross Council 117
Perth College 96
Perthshire Advertiser 8
Perthshire Courier 18

Queen Victoria 31

Reformation 20
Rigg, Rev. George 6, 7, 8, 9, 11, 12, 13, 18, 20, 21, 28, 43, 101, 120

Scarlet Fever 16, 52
School
    Attendance 15, 16, 17, 19, 26, 28
    Behaviour 15
    Class Sizes 10
    Curriculum 11
    Equipment 11
    Monitress 10
    Perth School Board 39
    Pupil Teachers 10, 35
    Qualified Teachers 10
    Qualifying Exam 69
    School Day 12
    School Inspectors 24, 110
    Unqualified Teachers 36
    Wet Weather 16
School Boards 22
School Inspector 36
School Leaving Age 52
School Manager 9
Scotsman 21
Sister Mary Elizabeth 14
Sister Mary Teresa 14
Smith, Mary Jane 14
St. John the Baptist 1, 4, 46, 105

St. John's Academy
    Badge and Tie   118
    Completion   118
    Name Chosen   117
    Start   118
St. John's School
    Accommodation Problems   40
    Alterations   86
    Announcement of New School   117
    Architecture   50
    As Local School   98
    Baby Boom, effects of   63
    Badge and Tie   105
    Balhousie Annexe   65, 86, 87
    Basement Rooms   49
    Class Sizes   36
    Corner House   60, 64, 86
    Corporal Punishment   72
    Decrease in Pupils   93
    Demolition of Original school   44
    Evacuees   54, 55
    Gym Facilities   40, 48, 86
    Kinloch Rannoch, Expeditions to   88
    Medical Report   33, 39
    Music and Drama   106
    Old Perth Academy Buildings   68
    Open Air   51
    Opening in 1938   46
    Original Site   43
    Outdoor Activities, Dalguise   103
    Overcrowding   52, 60, 63, 97
    Parent Teacher Association   86, 89, 96
    Plans at 1902   31
    Playground   48
    Pupils from Poland   119
    Pupils' Lavatories   32, 40
    Pupils' Physiques   34
    Pupils, Shortage of   88
    Raising of School Leaving Age 1947   64
    Selection at Age Eleven   69
    Separate Playgrounds   33
    Staffing problems   35
    Transport Dispute   93
St. John's Toun of Perth   1
St. Luke's Fair   16

Stewart, John   9
Stormont, Earls of   14
Stuart, Dr. Charles   33
Stuart, Marie T.   86

Tattie howkin'   17
Tayside Regional Council   93
Tullimet   28
Typhoid   16

Ursuline Sisters   13, 14, 18, 21

Vatican   20

Walker, Alex HMI   24, 26
Walsall, West Midlands   29
Ward, James   78, 83, 84
Wild West   5
Willing, Steve   106
World War One   38
World War Two   42, 52, 63